T0068175

Song

IN THE NIGHT

MATHEW PHILIP

WESTBOW
PRESS®
A DIVISION OF THOMAS NELSON
& ZONDERVAN

WestBow Press books may be ordered through booksellers or by contacting:

WestBow Press
A Division of Thomas Nelson & Zondervan
1663 Liberty Drive
Bloomington, IN 47403
www.westbowpress.com
844-714-3454

All Scripture quotations are taken from The Holy Bible, New International Version®, NIV® Copyright © 1973, 1978, 1984, 2011 by Biblica, Inc.® Used by permission. All rights reserved worldwide.

Some stories or news pieces in the book are from my memories of reading other books or online postings or from listening to speakers.

ISBN: 978-1-6642-5680-4 (sc)
ISBN: 978-1-6642-5682-8 (hc)
ISBN: 978-1-6642-5681-1 (e)

Library of Congress Control Number: 2022902069

Print information available on the last page.

WestBow Press rev. date: 02/23/2022

CONTENTS

CONTENTS

ACKNOWLEDGMENTS

This book is a product of reflecting on my life and the life of friends and family members who shared their experiences. Writing songs and singing them have a unique way of strengthening our spirits and souls in transition times. Particularly, when the times are hard and you see obstacles everywhere, songs can help you not to give up and to get through adversity and challenges. Life is made of important markers whether it is starting school, getting married, having children, starting a new job, or retirement. Then there are other markers that are not as exciting but are painful in many cases. Diagnosis of a serious illness, starting therapies, and losing a life partner are all markers that that make up the big journey. Each stage in life can be exciting as well as challenging. Many heroes in history have written songs or poetry while going through pain and sorrow. If you may sing songs to the wind, to the storm, or to the fiery furnace in front of you, you can experience a special feeling of calm and comfort. Our sweetest songs are those that come out from the painful experiences of life.

"We look before and after,
And pine for what is not:
Our sincerest laughter
With some pain is fraught;
Our sweetest songs are those that
tell of saddest thought.
("To a Skylark," a poem by Percy Byshe Shelley)

I am grateful to those who were sincere in sharing their life stories that became part of this book. I am greatly indebted to the publishers who have put in their time and effort to proofread and correct spelling mistakes and grammatical errors.

The book would not have been possible without Evangeline, my wife and beloved fellow traveler in life's journey; together we made numerous mile markers along the highway of life. I am thankful for her insight in designing the cover and selecting the cover picture. I am indebted to my grandparents and parents who ingrained in me a deep-rooted faith. I am also thankful for several mentors, teachers, and random acquaintances who supported with great ideas and guidance.

INTRODUCTION

The great preacher C. H. Spurgeon wrote, "No matter how dark the night is, there is always something to sing about, even concerning that night." Sometimes in our darkest moments we need a song. It takes courage and a deep faith to be able to sing in the darkness. We all have nights that bring times of darkness in our lives—nights of sorrow, grief, brokenness, disappointments, anxiety, and the list goes on. At such times, if we stay closer to God, we can hear songs of encouragement and comfort that come amid such darkness.

During time of darkness and evil, we may wonder, "If God exists, why is there so much evil or suffering?" If you feel like God is silent today, trust on what God is preparing for tomorrow. It is not what happens after the pain that matters, it is how you get through the pain as it happens. If you experience a lack of response from God, that is the time that God has trusted you with a silence. The apparent silence from God is the sign that He is bringing you to a marvelous understanding of Himself. We can trust Him even when He is silent. Then we can change the question to: "If God doesn't exist, why there is so much beauty in the world?" which will in turn bring songs of joy and victory among moments of sorrow and grief.

CHAPTER 1

Life Is a Gift

Receiving an unmerited gift is always exciting and joyful. Life is a gift from God. We did not come to this world by our choice. My birth and death are not my choices. Many of the painful situations are not our choices. But when we go through them, we get a new perspective in life. We start to question, What is my purpose in life? Whom do I love? What things are important? What are my priorities? The answers to these questions become more real at the painful times of life. God has not promised us long and pain-free lives. If we trust that God is good, we can see His amazing work of redemption of our situations of brokenness.

Life is a gift that cannot be boxed in a gift wrap. It cannot be purchased or leased. It is one magnificent gift that is not valued based on the size, shape, or color of the box. Its meaning comes from the value that the recipient assumes as well as the value that the giver establishes. The most precious gifts are not boxes filled with stuff but sweet presents that hold so much more: love, gratitude, and kindness. These things make up the most beautiful gift that we call life. This book is written based on personal experiences and stories of others with the hope of becoming a guidepost in the journey of life where one can sing the notes of harmony in the middle of discords of doubts and anxiety.

Dan, who received a kidney transplant, shared his story on how a disease caused unspeakable havoc on everything he loved and knew. When he discovered that both of his kidneys were dead due to cancer, he was confronted with some difficult questions about the realities of living with chemo and dialysis, the possibility of having a replacement procedure, and what the near and distant future might look like. After his fight with many infections, he was selected for kidney replacement surgery. "I broke into tears because my life is a beautiful gift, and the people I have in my life make it more beautiful," he said. But today he celebrates each victory: climbing the steps, singing songs, and making any progress on his battle against cancer. Every small accomplishment in a day is an immeasurable and invaluable gift that cannot be replaced or boxed inside a gift box. Our lives are made up of single breaths at a time that are filled with the love and grace of God.

Just as it is important to follow the signs and markers on a highway, it is good to know the markers that make up the journey of our lives. A group of young people were on an adventurous journey on the highway. A patrol officer stopped them and told the driver that they were going too slow on the seventy-five-mile-per-hour highway; the minimum speed limit was forty, and they were going twenty.

The young driver pointed to the highway sign and said, "It says twenty."

The officer said, "Young man, that is the highway number and not the speed limit."

The friends in the back seat then gasped in shock and said, "Thank you, officer. We just got off Highway 130."

Mile markers are real, and they have to be paid attention to. Some people pay attention to speed limits only when they see a police car. There are markers that show us how many miles we've passed or how many miles we have to travel to our destination. If you were driving on a lonely highway at night, and your car broke down, you would probably call someone for assistance, such as the police. But did you ever stop to think how you would tell them where you are? Telling them you are on Highway 50 near the bridge with the big pillars probably is not going to help all that much. It also probably won't be that helpful if you tell them that you are about fifteen to twenty miles from the nearest town with an old red barn. If you can tell them you are closer to mile marker 21, though, you will probably get the assistance you need fairly quickly. Each mile marker in the journey of life is a spot to stop and rejoice because of the significance it gives us in the direction of life.

Paul Gerhardt was a pastor who lived in seventeenth-century Germany. The Thirty Years' War had brought devastation all across the country. His wife and four children died within a span of a few years. The conflicts within the church and political pressures filled his life with distress. Despite great suffering, he wrote more than 130 hymns, many of them characterized by a rejoicing spirit. One of Gerhardt's hymns, "Holy Spirit, Source of Gladness," contains this verse:

> Let that love which knows no measure
> Now in quickening showers descend,
> Bringing us the richest treasures
> Man can wish or God can send;
> Hear our earnest supplication,
> Every struggling heart release;
> Rest upon this congregation,
> Spirit of untroubled peace.

Because God's abounding love is poured into our hearts by the Holy Spirit (Romans 5:5), there is no situation in life where we cannot experience the joy from God.

CHAPTER 2

Song in the Night

Different people find different places to sing their solos. Some sing in bathrooms, and some sing while being alone. I have heard people singing while cooking in the kitchen or doing laundry. It is not uncommon to see people driving and singing madly and loudly, with a lot of animation as well. Some like to sing in the crowds.

Joe liked to sing in the choir. But he was always off beat and off notes. He had a beat of his own, and it was affecting the choir as a whole. The efforts of the choir director to get him out of the choir were fruitless. Joe thought he was doing a fantastic job and was so excited to be part of the choir. So finally, the choir director approached the pastor. The pastor called Joe and said, "I think you are a good fit for leading the children's church. I need you to take that responsibility."

Joe said, "No, Pastor, that is the time when the choir sings, and I cannot miss the choir."

The pastor then asked him to take up an usher position that he immediately refused: "You know I sing in the choir, and I cannot miss it."

After trying several things, the pastor said, "Joe, some people have told me that you can't sing, and you need to get out of the choir."

Joe was shocked. He paused for a moment and replied, "Pastor, several people have told me that you can't preach." Singing in a choir is not as easy as singing in a crowd.

The psalmist who wrote Psalm 42 is talking about singing in the dark of night. Singing in daylight is common. Singing in good times is easy, but singing in the dark moments is not. The message of this psalm is that to brood on sorrow is to be broken and disheartened, but if we look up to God, we can sing even on the darkest day. Singing songs of praise to God will bring light amid darkness. God will become our countenance that shines on our faces.

Singing in the dark is not easy. Charles H. Spurgeon said, "It is easy to sing when we can read the notes by daylight; but the skillful singer is he who can sing when there is not a ray of light to read by." It is hard to sing when you cannot see the notes. The darkness seems to hide the notes of life. A friend of ours talked about the continued troubles she has in her life. She lost her job, and then after a few weeks, she was diagnosed with some issues that needed surgery, and they would not schedule and set up a date for the surgery because of COVID-19. Her uncle passed away of COVID-19 with nobody around him to bury him. His wife and the only son were in the ICU, both infected with the flu. She showed a picture of a minister and the two funeral home people fully covered in hazard suits doing his burial. She said, "I don't see the light at the end of the tunnel for this family."

We all go through periods of darkness in our lives at one point or another. Dark nights of exhaustion and weakness, nights of doubt and anxiety, nights of bewilderment and fear, and nights of oppression or injustice are part of life. A friend of our family talked about the continued hardships he and his wife face in their life. Both husband and wife are successful dentists running their own practice. The wife's dad passed away unexpectedly a couple of months ago, leaving the mother alone, and she had to move in with them. Shortly after that, the husband's dad was diagnosed with an advanced stage of cancer. His mom died a few years ago, and he is the only child. They have brought him down with them to start treatment at the cancer center and are now taking care of him. Now they have two older people in their home to care for, along with their two young children under ten years old. When they talked to me, one of them said, "We have always been on the short end of life. We spent over a decade in the military; we both went to dental schools, and now we've started a practice. We work hard six days a week for over ten hours a day, and we're taking care of two young children. When are we going to get a break and see light? I guess it is our time of darkness we need to get through."

Why do birds sing? Because they can and they will.

Similarly, we can sing songs if we have the will. In Psalm 42, the sons of Korah find things that are not getting better. "Deep calls to deep" (Psalm 42:7) alludes to things that may seem to be going from bad to worse. But the psalm does not end there; it continues with the trust in a living God who loves despite our conditions. "By day the Lord directs his love, at night his song is with me—a prayer to the God of my life" (Psalm 42:8).

Acts 16:20–25 records how Paul and Silas were severely beaten and cast into the dark Philippian jail for preaching the message of Jesus Christ, a custom unlawful for Romans to accept or practice. They had been severely flogged and thrown into prison, and the jailer was commanded to guard them carefully. "When he received these orders, he put them in the inner cell and fastened their feet in the stocks. About midnight Paul and Silas were praying and singing hymns to God, and the other prisoners were listening to them. Suddenly there was such a violent earthquake that the foundations of the prison were shaken. At once all the prison doors flew open, and everyone's chains came loose. The jailer woke up, and when he saw the prison doors open, he drew his sword and was about to kill himself because he thought the prisoners had escaped. But Paul shouted, "Don't harm yourself! We are all here!" The jailer called for lights, rushed in, and fell trembling before Paul and Silas. He then brought them out and asked, "Sirs, what must I do to be saved?" They replied, "Believe in the Lord Jesus, and you will be saved—you and your household." Then they spoke the word of the Lord to him and to all the others in his house. At that hour of the night the jailer took them and washed their wounds; then immediately he and all his household were baptized. The jailer brought them into his house and set a meal before them; he was filled with joy because he had come to believe in God—he and his whole household."

Paul and Silas found themselves in a difficult place when they were imprisoned for telling others about Jesus. But discomfort didn't dampen their faith. "About midnight Paul and Silas were praying and singing hymns to God, and the other prisoners were listening to them" (Acts16:25). Their bold worship created the opportunity to continue to talk about Jesus. "Then they spoke the word of the Lord to him and to all the others in his house" (Acts 16:32).

In the summer of 1963, after an all-night bus ride, US civil rights activist Fannie Lou Hamer and six other black passengers stopped to eat at a diner in Winona, Mississippi. After law enforcement officers forced them to leave, they were arrested and jailed. But the humiliation would not end with unlawful arrest. All received severe beatings, but Fannie's was the worst. After a brutal attack that left her near death, she burst out in song: "Paul and Silas was bound in jail, let my people go." And she did not sing alone. Other prisoners, restrained in body but not in soul, joined her in worship.

Most of us will not likely face the extreme circumstances encountered by Paul, Silas, or Fannie, but each of us will face uncomfortable situations. When that happens, our strength comes from our faithful God. May there be a song in our hearts that will honor Him and give us the boldness to speak for truth—even amid trouble.

In the darkness of pain and suffering, God's people can sing songs of praise. It will transform the world around them. One who can sing songs of empowerment in the night when we feel powerless will be able to sing the song of victory during the day. Jesus sang on the night before He went to the Garden of Gethsemane. Toward the final days of ministry while Jesus was getting ready to be crucified, He spent the day with His disciples and celebrated the last supper. Jesus took bread, and when He had given thanks, He broke it and gave it to His disciples, saying, "Take and eat; this is my body." Then He took a cup, and when he had given thanks, He gave it to them, saying, "Drink from it, all of you. This is my blood of the covenant, which is poured out for many for the forgiveness of sins. I tell you, I will not drink from this fruit of the vine from now on until that day when I drink it new with you in my Father's kingdom" (Matthew 26:27–28). He knew that one of His own disciples would betray Him. We read that they sang in the middle of that confusing and difficult night. "When they had sung a hymn, they went out to the Mount of Olives" (Matthew 26:30). Jesus predicted that Peter was going to deny Him, and Judas was going to betray Him. Yet we see Him singing a hymn amid dark and weak moments.

Fanny Crosby has been called "The Songbird in the Dark." Though blinded in infancy, she wrote hymns that inspirationally envision our future reunion with Christ. Early in her life, Fanny had a dream in which she saw the panorama of a glorious heaven, and many of her songs reflect that theme. By the time of her death, she had penned at least eight thousand hymns.

Songs such as "Tell Me the Story of Jesus" and "To God Be the Glory" are still popular today. "Blessed Assurance" is one the sweetest of all these that I love to sing. If you feel like you are imprisoned in situations outside of your control, that is the time to sing praises to God who can give you a song in the night.

For the saints, the sweetest songs often come from the darkest nights. The Psalmist Asaph said, "I thought about the former days, the years of long ago; I remembered my songs in the night" (Psalm 77:5–6). Asaph considered the extent of his cry to God, remembered what God had done in ancient times. He wondered why God, who seemed to answer sooner in the past, now takes a long time. His psalm is a song of hope in the middle of darkness of hopelessness.

Apostle Paul was taken as a prisoner to Rome along with other prisoners in a ship. In the middle of the sea, they encountered a big storm by the name Northeaster. In Acts 27, we read about him singing praises to God in the middle of the night when the storm was threatening their lives. "Just before dawn Paul urged them all to eat. "For the last fourteen days," he said, "you have been in constant suspense and have gone without food—you haven't eaten anything. Now I urge you to take some food. You need it to survive. Not one of you will lose a single hair from his head. After he said this, he took some bread and gave thanks to God in front of them all. Then he broke it and began to eat" (Acts 27:33–35). We read that they were all encouraged by the praising and thanksgiving service in the middle of a life-threatening situation.

On March 30, 1899, a Maundy Thursday, a British ship by

name Stella sank in the middle of the night with147 passengers and forty-three crew members. The ship sank in just eight minutes. Seventy-seven people died in that wreck. There were only four lifeboats. Rescue ships were sent from the shore, but because of fog, the ships could not see their way. There were twelve women in a lifeboat that wandered in the darkness. Margaret Williams (Greta Williams), a young woman, was among them. She started singing the song based on Psalm 69: "O rest in the Lord, wait patiently for Him—He shall give thee thy heart desires—commit thy way unto him. Fret not but trust Him." In the beginning she was singing alone. After a few minutes, a couple joined and later more and more joined. They all sang with a loud voice amid the gloomy darkness in the wild sea. Their song became louder and louder as the midnight darkness became darker. The rescue ships wandering in the fog were able to pick up a feeble noise of song in the darkness. They steered in the direction of that noise and rescued them after fourteen hours of floating around in the darkness. The night was filled with the song of hope, which became the song of rescue.

Illness, broken relationships, loss of loved ones, conflicts, stress, and many other challenges can bring darkness. Sometimes we may feel overwhelmed and discouraged. But as Christians, we can look forward with hope. Because of Christ's death and resurrection, we can live with the assurance that the best is yet to come. We can look forward to an eternal life of joy and peace with our Lord and Savior. It is often in our darkest times of discouragement and disappointment that God makes

His presence known most clearly. During our sufferings and troubles, He is our only source of strength. Put yourself in God's hands. Wait for His timing. He will give you a "song in the night."

For most of his adult life, German composer Ludwig van Beethoven's hearing gradually faded to the point where he could communicate only by means of writing. To everyone's amazement, it was after Beethoven lost his hearing that he wrote some of his greatest masterpieces. Shut out from the distractions of the world, new melodies and harmonies flooded in upon him as fast as his pen could write. His deafness had become a blessing. So too, children of God often find new joy in their night of sorrow and unexpected grace in their time of need. When God shuts us away from the things of this world, we may expect to hear more perfectly the matchless harmonies of heaven.

CHAPTER 3

Songs of Saints

Do you know God sings? Zephaniah, a minor prophet who lived in the kingdom of Judah around 620 BC, wrote that the Lord God will rejoice with singing over His people. The prophet masterfully drew a picture with his words in which he described God as a musician who loves to sing for and with His children. He wrote: "The Lord your God is with you, the Mighty Warrior who saves. He will take great delight in you; in his love he will no longer rebuke you, but will rejoice over you with singing" (Zephaniah 3:17). God promised to be present forever with those who have been transformed by His mercy. But it does not stop there! He invites His people and joins with them to "be glad and rejoice with all your heart" (Zephaniah 3:14).

The Bible is full of songs to celebrate victories. One of them is Miriam's song. She is the sister of Moses who started singing after their escape through the Red Sea where God parted the waters and led them through on the dry land. "Then Miriam the prophet, Aaron's sister, took a timbrel in her hand, and all the women followed her, with timbrels and dancing." The book of Exodus talks about the deliverance from bondage. Miriam sang to them: "Sing to the Lord, for he is highly exalted. Both horse and driver he has hurled into the sea" (Exodus 15:20–21).

The people of Israel lived in Egypt over four hundred years. They ended up settling there because of Joseph, who had entered the country as a slave and then risen to a high position in the Egyptian government. Because of God's grace, the people had not only been preserved there, but had greatly prospered. Problems began when, perhaps a century later, a new pharaoh came onto the throne who did not know Joseph and all the good that he had done for Egypt. Instead, this pharaoh comes to see the Israelites as a possible threat. He subjects the Israelites as his slaves. He lays heavier burdens on them, and even begins to exterminate them, throwing their babies into the Nile. The Israelites suffered in slavery for several hundred years: a hard and hurtful existence, with the constant threat of death. But in the midst of their misery, a savior is born: Moses, the man of God. He was thrown into the Nile River by his own mother to escape his being killed as a baby by Pharaoh's soldiers. He was eventually rescued from the Nile by the daughter of Pharaoh and was raised by her in the palace. God was preparing him for a greater cause than himself.

Something great was about to unfold. Sure enough, God

appears to Moses and makes him Israel's great deliverer. Through him, God performs great signs and wonders, and He inflicts ten terrible plagues on the land, to break Pharaoh's stubborn will. Finally, after one last plague—the death of Egypt's firstborn—Pharaoh relents, and the people of Israel are allowed to leave. They are on their way at last to the "Promised Land" until Pharaoh comes to his "senses" and decides to chase them. The chase ended at the Red Sea, where the people of God walked through dry land and got to the other side while the soldiers of Pharaoh who followed them were drowned in that very sea. The people of God then had a big celebration with singing and dancing. With timbrel in hand, Miriam takes the lead in the chorus, and all the women joined her singing and dancing. It was also a celebration of God's deliverance from the Egyptian army as they passed through the Red Sea, and their enemies were swept away. Moses recorded two songs in praise of God's faithfulness and deliverance of the Israelites—one in Exodus 15 and the other one in Deuteronomy 32 when he was nearing his death. Moses saw the great deliverance that God provided from destruction. It was not because of their might and power that they were delivered but because of God's faithfulness and mercy.

Miriam's song was a song of preservation. She is called a prophetess in this context. Other women are described in the Bible as prophetesses, such as Deborah, Huldah, and Isaiah's wife, and in the New Testament, we can see the prophetess Anna, and Philip's four daughters. We don't know what Miriam did as prophetess, outside of this one event. But a prophet is someone who speaks God's Word to His people. And that is exactly what Miriam was doing: she was proclaiming His Word to His glory. While it is not clear exactly what kind of role she had in Israel, Miriam did have an important place. God said through the prophet Micah: "I brought you up out of Egypt and redeemed you from the land of slavery. I sent Moses to lead you, also Aaron and Miriam" (Micah 6:4). Miriam was counted among the leaders of God's people! So, on this day of victory, Miriam the prophetess would lift her voice and lead the nation in worship. She combined her "prophesying" with music. It was the song of Miriam that prophesied that a remnant will eventually be preserved.

Many of the psalms were written and sang as songs of pilgrimages. They sing about the important events in their journey as well as the greatness and mercies of God.

When Moses and Miriam sang, they did not only celebrate the past, but they also looked forward. They were singing about a Canaan that would be their new home: "You will bring them in and plant them on the mountain of your inheritance—the place, Lord, you made for your dwelling, the sanctuary, Lord, your hands established" (Exodus 15:17). This deliverance was one more step along the way, another step toward that place where God can again dwell among his people—like He did in the Garden of Eden. That's what God is working on, so be sure that He will bring us there, even if He must carry us the whole way. He will finish in us what He started. And that good news points us unmistakably to Christ the Savior. That is why the song of Moses and Miriam is also known as song of preservation or song of salvation.

A second truth that is seen so beautifully is God's preservation of the saints. He had done everything to save them, then shielded them from danger. He had done it so that He could bring them to the land of promise! God had led His people out, so He could lead them back into His holy presence.

Jesus's victory on the cross is so much greater than what happened at the Red Sea. While we were stuck in our sin, held captive by our fear of death, and there was no way out, Christ died for us. By His cross, and His resurrection, Christ released us from our chains of bondage to sin and death. Now He is carrying us through the life in this world toward our everlasting home. He has triumphed gloriously, and all the blessings of His victory belong to us! Like Miriam, we have the rights to sing and dance. Paul says, "In all these things we are more than conquerors through Him who loved us" (Romans 8:37). When we find ourselves weak and threatened, remember God's faithfulness is new every morning.

We see saints singing a song of victory in the book of Revelation. In Revelation 15:3, we see a song called: "The Song of Moses and the Song of the Lamb." It is sung by the great multitude of believers who were victorious of the devil and standing by the sea, and they're holding harps. They are not standing at the Red Sea, but at the "Crystal Sea." The great deliverance under Moses was a foreshadowing of the great deliverance that was accomplished by the true Lamb of God— Jesus Christ—whose blood must be applied by faith, to the heart of every man and woman who desires to be spared the wrath of God and delivered from His enemies (Exodus 15:1–18; Deuteronomy 31:30, 32:43).

The Song of the Lamb emphasizes the redemptive work and plan of God in Christ and His promise of deliverance through Christ's shed blood on the cross. Both songs, the "Song of Moses" and the "Song of the Lamb," are the response of grateful hearts celebrating God's merciful deliverance and a hopeful future. The song is about a hope of future in the presence of God. And together they sing, "Great and marvelous are your deeds, Lord God Almighty. Just and true are your ways, King of the nations" (Revelation 15:3). That is the keynote theme of scripture and of our lives: the great and marvelous works of our God, who in Christ has redeemed us from sin and death. So let that be our chorus and our refrain, each day of our lives.

A number of saints who lived in history had sung songs—Moses and Miriam, Job and David, Jesus and His disciples, Paul and Silas, John and Charles Wesley, Fanny Crosby and many others. Paul and Silas sang in prison when their chains were broken. Job sang in his affliction where he was strengthened. David sang in the middle of loneliness in the desert when he was comforted. Apostles sang in their trials of faith where they were confirmed in their hope. Martin Luther and John and Charles Wesley were all singing saints in history known to the Western World. There are those like Evangelist Kochukunju, K. V. Simon, Mosa Valsalam and many others in India who are known for singing songs of faith amid troubles. Their songs celebrate God's miraculous deliverance from the hard and mundane to a life of peace and joy. They all sang about a hopeful future.

God expresses His joy with singing when a sinner repents and becomes part of the heavenly kingdom. If anyone is in Christ, he is a new creation—Jesus said there will be great joy in heaven at the repentance of a sinner. That's why angels sang at the birth of the savior: "He set my feet on a rock and gave me a firm place to stand. He put a new song in my mouth, a hymn of praise to our God" (Psalm 40:2–3). The Bible says that at creation time, the stars were singing. We can call it the song of creation as described in the book of Job: "while the morning stars sang together and all the angels shouted for joy" (Job 38:7). A new creation brings songs of joy and celebration.

There is a lot of singing in heaven by various groups. According to the revelation given by John, four groups are mentioned as having harps in heaven: living creatures, elders (Revelation 5:8), heavenly singers (Revelation 14:2), and the tribulation saints (Revelation 7:10–14). The harps have a privileged position before God's throne. They contribute greatly to the heavenly harmony of the chorus that the redeemed offer to God. Often those who have been persecuted the most worship the most. Typically, it is because these saints arrive at the realization that they have nothing or no one but God. The things of this world pass away. They are seen as fleeting and empty. But praising God is eternal. We can only imagine the day when we will be together with God and with all those who have put their trust in Jesus as their Savior. How amazing it will be to hear our heavenly Father singing songs for and with us and experience His love, approval, and acceptance.

Thomas Andrew Dorsey (1899–1993) was an African American jazz musician from Atlanta. In 1932 while Dorsey was leading a church service, a man came onto the platform to hand him a telegram—his wife had just died in childbirth. Within twenty-four hours, his newborn baby died also. Thomas quickly spiraled downward into the depths of despair, doubting the goodness of God and determining never to write another hymn. It was the darkest time of his life when God seemed to be out of reach. A week after that horrible, life-changing day, Thomas was deep into his grief; he was sitting alone at a piano, in a friend's music room. Into the room came a heavy peace such as he had never known before. As that peace enveloped him, the words came to him: "Precious Lord, Take My Hand." Thomas felt the urge to play the piano began to well up from his heart and to spill out of his mouth. God had given him a song that would not only lift him from despair but would also change the course of his music career. The song goes like this: "Precious Lord, take my hand, Lead me on, let me stand. I am tired, I am weak, I am worn. Through the storm, through the night, Lead me on to the light; Take my hand precious Lord, lead me home ..."

CHAPTER 4

Changing Tunes with Changing Seasons

The tones and tunes of our songs may change with the change of seasons of life. The changing of the seasons is striking with beauties. Spring brings growth with new life and flowers; summer brings outside activities; fall has beautiful falling leaves of varied colors, and winter, though generally darker and colder, brings Christmas and festivities. Like nature, God has blessed us with seasons in life. A person born as an infant grows into a youth, then as an adult and pass through middle age and then to old age. Each season is a blessing because you had a chance to live up to that time.

Our lives are full of seasons—seasons of weather, seasons of events, seasons of age, and so on. When you were younger, you thought in fractions: "How old are you?" "I'm four and a half." When you are older it is like the weather, in whole numbers. You're never thirty-six and a half, or fifty and a half. You get into your teens, now they can't hold you back. You jump to the next number. "How old are you?" "I'm going to be sixteen." Oh, you might actually be only thirteen, but that's okay. You're going to be sixteen! You can't wait to drive. And then the greatest day of your life happens: you become twenty-one. Even the words sound like a ceremony—you "become" twenty-one. Yes! No more stamping on your driver's license. But then you turn thirty. Oh, what happened here? He "turned." What changed? You "become" twenty-one, then you "turn" thirty, and then you start "pushing" forty. Life is slipping away. Then you "reach" fifty. "Where are my dreams?" Next, you "make it" to sixty. "I didn't think I would make it." After you "make it" to sixty, you picked up so much speed that before you know what happened, you "hit" seventy! After that, it's a day-by-day thing. You no longer speak of "hitting" each year. Rather, your goals become much more immediate. You speak of "hitting" Wednesday, for example. Why, by the time you get into your eighties, it's a great accomplishment just to "hit" the next day. And it doesn't end there. Whereas in your teens you were always looking forward to the next year, by the time you get into your nineties you start looking backward: I was just ninety-two. Then a strange thing happens; if you make it over one hundred, you become a little kid again. "I'm one hundred and a half!" Yes, age is a funny thing.

A young child once asked a woman how old she was. She

answered, "thirty-nine and holding." The child thought for a moment, then said, "And how old would you be if you let go?" Most people do not want to acknowledge that they are getting older, even though that is the truth. The world seems to worship youth and is terrified of aging. Old people try to look and act young. In the United States, it is a $5 billion industry that caters to the makeup and hair dye business. The modern society has become mostly self-centered and utilitarian where people are looked upon with monetary value. Former Colorado Governor Richard Lamm said in a discussion of spiraling health care costs that terminally ill elderly people have "a duty to die and get out of the way." He apologized later. We see heroes as youthful and perfect in form. We don't see Superman or Batman portrayed with thick glasses, nor do we see them with receding hair or with wrinkles upon their face. Youth and vigor can become dangerous when used without drawing from the experience and wisdom of old age. George Bernard Shaw once said cynically, "Youth is a wonderful thing. What a crime to waste it on children."

When we are young, we can't wait to grow up to settle down after all the problems are resolved. We can remember while in college thinking that all our problems would be solved after graduation! A degree student said, "If I can just get out of this school, which is holding me captive, if I can get a degree and a wife, then I can ride off into the sunset." But our target moves as we grow older. When the kids go to college, we think we can settle down and enjoy smooth sailing from there. Not a chance. You get into your forties, "midlife crisis" kicks in followed by onset of physical problems. "Middle age is when your age starts to show around your middle," said Bob Hope, the famous American comedian of the last generation. Old age comes with its own problems. You start losing the big circle of friends you once had. Your children and friends who were constantly present in your life have moved away. You look back on old photographs, and you miss the days when you could jump high, run fast, or throw a ball far! The longer you live, your friends start leaving you to heaven, and you end up having more friends up there in heaven than you have here on earth.

There is a reason why God put seasons in our life. "There is a time for everything, and a season for every activity under the heavens" (Ecclesiastes 3:1). We gradually lose the strength and beauty that is temporary, so we'll be sure to concentrate on the strength and beauty that is eternal. And so, we'll be eager to leave the temporary, deteriorating part of us and be truly homesick for our eternal home. If we stayed young and strong and beautiful, we might never want to leave. Mark Twain said, "Life would be infinitely happier if we could only be born at the age of eighty and gradually approach eighteen." But who wants to die at the young age of eighteen? It is interesting to observe the people who refuse to accept old age. It's obvious from the lines on their faces and the furrows in their foreheads but looks odd with a heavily dyed dark beard and full hair. It is a physical impossibility to escape the reality of old age. It is a natural progression of life. It doesn't matter how many vitamins you take, or how well you watch your diet, or how much you exercise, you can't stop yourself from getting old! George Burns, the comedian who died at the age of one hundred, said, "You know you are getting old when your children start to look middle-aged."

The psalmist who wrote Psalm 71 is considered to be an older man toward the "prime time" of life. He prays, "Since my youth, God, you have taught me, and to this day I declare your marvelous deeds" (Psalm 71:17). The psalmist did not allow himself to sink into a sea of self-pity. He is not naming these problems to wallow in regrets or to live in the past or to be jealous of the young generation. Rather, he saw problems as a way of pointing his eyes to a more powerful and faithful God. Old age is called "prime time" in certain parts of the world and old people are called "seniors" or "prime timers." They have a rich and rewarding experience to learn and talk about the vast experience in life, which others do not have. God has reserved special benefits and special responsibilities for those who hold a head full of white or gray hair that shows a lifetime of lessons learned. "Gray hair is a crown of splendor" (Proverbs 16:31). Fall and winter are just as special to God as the spring season. A wise person once said: "Do not regret growing older. It is a privilege denied to many" (author unknown).

I heard a young man advising his father that the opposite of old is "new." He told a story:

> A little boy playing with his friends in the yard invited his grandmother to come and join. She said, "I'm too old to play those games now."

The boy looked up at her and asked, 'Grandma, when were you ever new?"

Moses was eighty years old when he began to lead Israel. Abraham was seventy-five years of age as he obeyed God's command to leave Haran to start on a long journey to Canaan.

The great evangelist John Wesley rode 350,000 miles on horseback, preaching the gospel of Jesus Christ. He preached over forty thousand different sermons. At the age of eighty-three, he complained because he could only study the Bible for fifteen hours a day. At the age of eighty-six, he became concerned about his spiritual state because he could not get up at 3:00 a.m. for his personal devotion. At eighty-seven, he learned his eleventh foreign language. And at eighty-eight, he was worried because he could only preach twice a day, six days a week.

Another great evangelist, George Muller, is said to have traveled two hundred thousand miles, using his linguistic ability to preach in several different languages to an estimated three million people around the world. However, Muller's statistics only began after his seventieth birthday and continued for the next seventeen years! Verdi penned his classic "Ave Maria" at age eighty-five; Michelangelo was eighty-seven when he completed "The Pietà," and Ronald Reagan became US president at seventy-five.

As Charles Spurgeon said, "they are highly favored who can like David, Samuel, Josiah, Timothy, and others say: Oh God, you are my trust from my youth." If God has taken seventy, eighty, or ninety years to train someone, He definitely has a greater plan for that person.

CHAPTER 5

Ebenezer: Thus Far God

E ach turn of event in our life has a different song we can all sing. We all have things that mark the special times in our lives. We all have milestones like birthdays, sweet sixteen, graduation, marriage, first job, first home, having children, their graduations, birth of the first grandchild, and the list goes on. Retirement, promotions, deaths, births, marriages—all are dubbed milestones because these events will change your life forever. Then there are those other occasions as sickness, loss of job or a dear one, move to another city, and so on. There were special people who marked those occasions with you. Some of the events are happy and some of them may not be good. Some of them may be milestones of upsets and failures. But through it all, we are being shaped into the character of who God wants us to be.

We can see the stages that little children go through as each stage of growth sets in. The first time turning over and then standing up and then walking are great markers of accomplishment children seem to be proud of. I am sure the parents and grandparents are proud cheerers on these as well. You can see the thrill and a sense of pride by looking at the face of a child when he or she starts to walk. Then comes the stage of first day in kindergarten and then school. I can remember the first day when my mother took me with her to the primary school in a local village. We bought new clothes and new school bag and supplies to get ready for that big day. As a five-year-old, I was more excited about the new stuff I can have than the school, since I did not know enough about what school was. Then came along the graduations, many of them—fifth grade, tenth grade, twelfth grade, and college. These are events that left a vivid memory carved in my heart as well as in the hearts of many dear ones.

One of the great memories I have is about my first day going to school. First grade in school is a great marker that stands out in our lives. I can remember still the first day when my mom dressed me up in new clothes to take me to the first grade in a remote village school in India. She was a teacher in the same school, and I was one of the privileged kids. I had my mom with me all the time, but at the same time, I had my limitations. Because mom was watching always, I could not do certain things others were able to do. But all that shaped me in the future years because of the formation of my childhood as a teacher's son. Good family and friends are gifts that will shape who you are.

The prophet Samuel set up a stone to commemorate the victory over the Philistines at Mizpah (1 Samuel 7:12). He called it "Ebenezer," which means "thus far the Lord has helped us." The experience of "Ebenezer" brings songs of gratitude that we all can sing at any turning point in life. Retirement, Social Security, old age, sickness, and death are important mile events. Some of them may be markers of successes and celebration while others can be of upsets and failures just like the highway mile markers can be in good and beautiful spots, while others are in lonely or wooded parts. Some are in dark areas, and some are in bright areas. But through it all, we are being shaped into the persons who we eventually become.

The world is not getting more spiritual, but the opposite. Gratitude for the blessings is not a concept that is getting approval among the newer generations. Nobody has to be grateful to anyone for the achievements and successes in life. A study by CNN in 2007 reported that 83 percent of people they polled said they never doubted the existence of God. That decreased to 68 percent in 2012. Data analysts studied by means of "Ngram," a software analytical tool that is used to build linguistic models, reported that faith in God has been decreasing for the last two centuries. Using this tool, you can run visualizations for bigrams and trigrams that start with pronouns. These visual comparisons allow us to see differences in how the two subjects are used—both where they are similar and diverge. For example, among the top 120 trigrams, "he" and "she" have many common second words. However, they differ on some interesting ones; for example, only "he" connects to "argues," while only "she" connects to "love." Stephen Prothero, a Boston University religion scholar and author, searched the Ngram database for the words "faith" and "doubt" in American English from 1800 to 2008. He found that during much of the early nineteenth century, "faith" won out over "doubt," but in the twentieth century "doubt" won over "faith." As we pass on, the need to leave a legacy of faith is now more important than ever to commit just like the psalmist to declare His power to the next generation. The truth is that our songs become sweeter as we grow older because they come from the experiences of life.

Gratitude or gratefulness is way down in the list of Ngram searches. Many have difficulty in acknowledging God as the source of our blessings. Accumulation of "stuff" in a materialistic world seems to be the measuring stick of blessings. The society feels entitled to what it has, or a person feels the right to be blessed, does not feel the need to show gratitude to anyone. A teenager used to sell lemonade for fifty cents in front of his house after school to make money for his personal expenses. A jogger used to go by twice a week and put fifty cents in his box without taking a cup of lemonade. This continued for several months, until one day the teenager stopped the jogger for a talk.

The jogger said, "I know you want to ask me why I never take a cup of lemonade after putting the money in your box."

The boy replied, "No, sir, I just wanted to tell you that the price of lemonade went up to sixty cents."

The recipients of gifts given by God feel a kind of entitlement when they know that they don't deserve it. Gratitude has no place when we see relationship as disposable; when we see everything through the lens of commercial business transactions. Just like gratitude is contagious, the lack of gratitude is also contagious and is passed from one generation to the next.

Songs of praises are often music of the soul filled with gratitude like David, who sang, "Praise the Lord, my soul; all my inmost being, praise his holy name. Praise the Lord, my soul, and forget not all his benefits" (Psalm 103:1–2).

If we fail to choose gratitude, the default is to choose ingratitude, which a lot of people choose every day. To quote the famous words of Abraham Lincoln, "We have grown in numbers, wealth and power, as no other nation has ever grown. But we have forgotten God. We have forgotten the gracious hand which preserved us in peace, and multiplied and enriched and strengthened us; and we have vainly imagined, in the deceitfulness of our hearts, that all these blessings were produced by some superior wisdom and virtue of our own. Intoxicated with unbroken success, we have become too self-sufficient to feel the necessity of redeeming and preserving grace, too proud to pray to the God that made us!" (http://www.abrahamlincolnonline.org/lincoln/speeches/fast.htm)

CHAPTER 6

Mile Markers

S inging during travel is very comforting and can be inspirational. When my wife and I visited Israel and Palestine, there were groups of travelers that were singing and enjoying their journey. We joined some of those groups and sang together mostly songs of thanksgiving and praises. Certain travel points are places where we would be prompted to write and sing songs. Someone in our group wrote a song inspired by the experience of visiting the garden of Gethsemane. We have markers on our journey of life where we have personal songs to sing.

Mile markers are stones buried on the sides of highways that help us to determine direction and distance when we travel. In the USA, they generally increase from the south to the north, and from the west toward east. The exit numbers are generally lined up with mile markers so that you can calculate how long you have traveled and how much distance is left to the destination. Without them, we become lost and vulnerable. If you call for emergency help, they will ask your location about your mile marker or exit number to get to you quickly.

These exit numbers give us a sense of comfort and peace in knowing where we are and what direction we are heading. The numbers either increase or decrease. You can find mile markers along all sorts of highways. Some are local or state highways, while others may be large interstate highways.

They can help you tell someone with some precision exactly where you are. On most highways, the mile markers also coordinate with the exit numbers. If you know you're headed for Exit 57 and you just passed mile marker 47, then you know you've got approximately ten miles to go until you reach your destination. In this way, mile markers can help you keep track of where you are and how far away you are from certain exits. Most highways change mile marker numbering at state borders. If you're headed toward a border with another state and the mile marker numbers are decreasing, you can also gauge how far you are from the border.

Mile markers on interstate highways can also help you determine which direction you are going. On most interstates, mile marker numbers begin at the south state line on north-south routes and increase as you travel north. On east-west routes, the numbers begin on the western state border and increase as you travel east. Some of these mile markers are in good and beautiful spots; others are in lonely or wooded parts. Some are in dark areas, and some are in bright areas. But without them, we become lost and vulnerable.

Unknowingly, they give us a sense of comfort and peace in knowing where we are and what direction we are heading. In the highway journey of life, there are mainly four groups of markers. Some are private, and others are public. Some are positive, and others are negative. You can imagine four quadrants, on a circle, the horizontal line being that divides good and bad and the perpendicular line divides between private and public. Then you can see them as good/private, good/public, bad/private, and bad/public that make the four quadrants. Life is made up of a large circle of these different types of quadrants of events.

The birth of a child is a great mile marker as the beginning of life in this world, but also it is a great marker for the parents. It is a marker in their journey that gave them a new decision point about child raising and planning. When a baby is born into this world, it is an unfamiliar place, with wind, heat, cold, talk of people etc. When the baby opens its eyes, he/she sees a group of strangers, who eventually become family.

Those strangers were the dear ones who were anxiously waiting for the child's appearance into this world, making sure he/she gets the greatest care and love and attention possible on this earth. To them, the baby is not a stranger but the beloved child that God has given them as a gift. That day is a mile marker in the journey of his/her life. It is also a mile marker for many others like grandparents, uncles, and aunts, and many others—in fact, for the world itself. The birth of a child has brought many other "births" in this world. A father and mother are born in this world. So are uncles, aunts, brothers, sisters, cousins, and the list goes on. The child brings new teachers, pastors, Sunday school teachers, friends, and many other relationships that did not exist before. I have a collection of old black and white photos of a number of new babies born in our family along with their parents and other relatives. You can see the excitement and the joy in their faces as they witness a new baby start life in this world.

Baptism is a mile marker in life when the church is gathered to witness the initiation of an individual into the family of church and God. The child is being welcomed to a larger family of God along with generations of others who have accepted the baptism. It is commendable that parents decide to baptize their children as an infant.

Many people may have different opinions about the kinds of baptisms, but all Christians everywhere agree on having baptized in water and the spirit. Some may say that they will wait till the children grow up and make decisions for themselves. We don't do that when it comes to sending our kids to school or taking them to the doctor or getting vaccinations. As parents, we make many decisions for our children in matters of health, safety, education, and many others.

Of course, they may later reject what we have done for them. But that possibility does not relieve us of the responsibility to do all that we can to bring them to the family of God. We should not wait for our children to decide about being in the family of

God just as we do not wait for them to decide if they would like to be a part of our human family.

There are two sacraments instituted by all Christian churches—baptism and Holy Communion—and both are acts of God. All other rites are called ordinances—based on human act. Both baptism and Holy Communion are witnessing to the means of the grace of God. They are both divine actions and not of man, and none of these sacraments is a ticket to heaven.

That is why how we administer baptism is not important, just like we differ in the way we take Holy Communion. Being a symbol, baptism is needed only one time. It does not matter if you are immersed or sprinkled or dipped or sprayed or wiped. It does not matter how long you are under water or who has done your baptism.

> He saved us, not because of righteous things we
> had done, but because of his mercy. He saved
> us through the washing of rebirth and renewal
> by the Holy Spirit, whom he poured out on us
> generously through Jesus Christ our Savior,
> so that, having been justified by his grace, we
> might become heirs having the hope of eternal
> life. (Titus 3:5–7)

Salvation is through the personal acceptance of Jesus Christ as Lord and savior. Baptism does not cleanse from sin; rather it is a witness to the cleansing. Jesus received baptism not for the remission of sin because He was sinless. He did so to identify with us.

Baptism declares the identity as a child of God. When Jesus was baptized in Jordan River, the Holy Spirit descended on Jesus at His baptism, and a voice came from heaven. Luke 3:22 and Mark 1:11 record the voice as addressing Jesus by saying "You are my beloved Son, in whom I am well pleased," while in Matthew 3:17, the voice seems to address the crowd "This is my beloved Son, in whom I am well pleased." I take it as it was addressed to Jesus as God's affirmation and the crowd that witnessed heard as declaration to them. Through baptism, God conveys to us our identity as God's beloved children, and we are precious to God. Jesus said, "Let the little children come to me" (Matthew 19:14). Faith is not merely a product of reason but relation. It is a relationship of love and trust, a relationship that is not limited to the mind, and children know love and trust more than adults. When Jesus commands His disciples to let the children come to Him and not hinder them, He is calling the disciples (and us) to do more than just step aside and hope kids make it to Jesus on their own. He is calling us to work to help children come to Christ. That responsibility falls on the shoulders of the parents as well as every disciple of Christ. We should feel a sense of urgency to reach out to those who have never been baptized. The church uses a time of baptism to remember each of our baptismal covenants that by dying with Jesus in baptism, we have a new life in Him. Through baptism we were buried with Christ and rose to life with Him. We repent of our sin, renounce the spiritual forces of wickedness, and reject the evil powers of this world. During baptism, we affirm that we will keep that person in our prayers and do everything possible to increase in faith, confirm in hope and raise him/ her in the knowledge and grace of God. This is a marker for declaring one's identity. We, who are all God's children by one baptism, are witnesses to this, and we trust that person into His mighty hands that no evil will touch or take him/her away from God ever.

A child's baptism is a mile marker in life as well as for the rest of the world. Baptism is an important sacrament for Christians that is not optional. It is not an act of humans, rather it is act of God. It is the acceptance of God's grace. The newly baptized have joined a larger spiritual family called "church." Just like everyone in one family has a matching blood characteristic called DNA, the persons have a spiritual blood characteristic because we all are saved by the blood of Jesus. Baptism is a witness about the identity of belonging to that family. The baptism is the occasion when the church welcomes you into the family! As seen in the gospel of Mark, the voice from heaven is addressed to Jesus in the first person: "You are my beloved Son, in whom I am well pleased" (Mark 1:11). Baptism teaches us who we are—God's beloved children—and confers upon us the promise of God's unconditional regard. God's beloved children. We belong to God's family, and baptism is a tangible sign of that. "He saved us, not because of righteous things we had done, but because of his mercy. He saved us through the washing of rebirth and renewal by the Holy Spirit" (Titus 3:5).

Baptism is first and foremost God's activity. That is one reason why we perform infant baptism. I commend the parents who choose to baptize their children at a very young age. Some may say that they will wait till the child grows up and acknowledges the need and decides for himself or herself about baptism. Remember, this is not an act of man and human decisions. It is an act of God where He bestows His grace.

Children are gifts. As parents, we are entrusted with the responsibility to attend to their needs even when they are young. Children are a gift from the Lord; they are a reward from God. Children born to a young man are like sharp arrows in a warrior's hands (Psalm 127:3–5). Christians should make every effort to help children to come to Christ. When Jesus commands His disciples to let the children come to Him and not hinder them, He's calling them (and us) to do more than just step aside and hope kids make it to Jesus on their own. He is calling us to work to help children come to Christ even as the parents were bringing their children to Christ. That responsibility falls first on the shoulders of the parents, but then it falls on us as a church.

Baptism declares the identity as a child of God. The Holy Spirit descended on Jesus at His baptism, and a voice came from heaven. At Jesus's baptism, a voice from heaven invariably announces to Jesus, "This is my Son, whom I love; with him I am well pleased" (Matthew 3:17). So also in our baptism, God conveys to us our identity as God's beloved children— children and people so precious to God. That is another reason I commend the family on baptizing this precious gift of God; it claims and declares to the world that this a child of God, and not of this world. Traditional Protestants, Catholics, and Orthodox Christians all baptize infants. It is not a human work to satisfy some religious ritual. Baptism suggests that we best understand "who" we are and "whose" we are. Our example is Jesus who was confirmed by the Holy Spirit and acknowledged by the Father even though John's baptism was for the remission of sin. Jesus didn't need to be baptized for the sake of sin but did so anyway so as to identify with us.

Baptism is not a "ticket to heaven" where parents want their children "done" just to be on the safe side. No, not at all. Baptism announces God's inclusion of us into God's family, and we feel some urgency to reach out to those who have never been baptized. The church that assembles to witness baptism takes up a big responsibility. With each child born to this world, the society and the spiritual community assume the role of caregivers. We learn a lot from children. There is a big change of our lives before we had kids and after we had kids. The perspective and outlook toward everything changed. The need to teach our children what we believe and why we believe it became very important. Many people like to dedicate their children in place of baptism. Dedication is a human act— something we pledge or give to God. Baptism is a divine act, a pledge and gift God gives to us. Baptism of infants includes the reaffirmation of the vows of the baptismal covenant by parents, sponsors, and the congregation; but chiefly it celebrates what God is doing and will do in the life of the infant. "Start children off on the way they should go, and even when they are old they will not turn from it" (Proverbs 22:6). Studies have shown that the majority of the people who became Christians did it by the age of twenty-five. After the age of the thirties, the statistics go down to less than one percent. The truth is that it is less likely to become a Christian once you get older. So, we need to rejoice and sing songs of praises at every mile marker of the faith journey.

CHAPTER 7

Beauty for Ashes

The greatest example of a man who sang praises to God amid abandonment and physical affliction of his body is the man named Job. He sings about redemption by a Redeemer who lives, who can redeem his situation. The book of Job is considered the oldest book in the Bible. "He was the greatest man among all the people of the East" (Job 1:3). He was the greatest, not only because he was very wealthy and well known at the time, but also "this man was blameless and upright; he feared God and shunned evil" (Job 1:1). He was a very successful man; people were inclined to think that he was a favorite of God's grace. Then suddenly and without any explanation or reason, everything collapsed in his life. It was like a tsunami or an earthquake shattered the foundation of his life. The messengers come one after the other with bad news that all is lost, and "I am the only one who has escaped to tell you" (Job 1:15). It was like some evil fate that there would always be a messenger to deliver the wrenching sad news to a victim. His livestock, all his seven sons and three daughters were gone in a great wind; all became a desert in front of him. The Bible says at this point that he "tore his robe and shaved his head. Then he fell to the ground in worship" (Job 1:20). I stand at awe of this scene of a man, in wretched shape, having lost all possessions including all his children, and instead of railing against God and his situation, Job bowed and worshipped.

In modern times, we can probably relate to Job when many middle-aged people go through what is called a midlife crisis. You must make many major decisions regarding career, children's college, their marriage, and so many other events crowd up together in the middle ages. Men must face what has come to be referred to as the "midlife syndrome." We reach those middle years when we begin to realize that most of what we intended to do has not yet been accomplished. And we can no longer deny the fact that the better part of life has been lived. Often at this crisis point men feverishly begin to build monuments by which they will be remembered.

When Job's body was afflicted, it became more intimate. He was infected with sores from foot to head. He now sits in the ashes, possibly due to some soothing effect or maybe that his wife and others asked him for fear of contamination. Job lost his companion's emotional and spiritual support; she suggests "Curse God and die" (Job 2:9). I don't think badly of Job's wife for saying this. In fact, I think well of her, a good woman, who saw it all and couldn't take it any longer to see the suffering of her darling love. His dear wife, who couldn't bear the sight, said that out of compassion and love. In fact, she was a faithful wife and mother. Then he is being visited by some close friends. They were well-meaning, trusted friends who had held him in high esteem in the past. They now come with words of wisdom. Though they mean well, they think that Job needs advice at this time. They try to convince Job that his misery is due to things he had done wrong in the past. His friends used their words to weaken his faith. Good friends are the ones who strengthen you in time of your weakness.

Job does not need a full ear of advice at this time. Job needs a sympathetic voice to listen to. They tell Job how it is that he has come to such a condition, and that he is suffering because he deserves it. As it happens to us sometimes, to find a reason or explanation to the situation. We mean well, but it could hurt more. Job calls them "miserable comforters" (Job 16:2). If you have been counseled by someone like this, pray that God gives you the strength to get through. Job laments to his friends that they are tormenting him more with their words. Job has lost the trust and respect of his trusted friends at this point. His servants do not want to come near him, probably due to the stench of his wounds. He says, "My relatives have gone away; my closest friends have forgotten me. My guests and my female servants count me a foreigner; they look on me as on a stranger. I summon my servant, but he does not answer, though I beg him with my own mouth. My breath is offensive to my wife; I am loathsome to my own family" (Job 19:14–17). Incidentally, we don't see brothers or sisters mentioned in the scene.

This is the point where a heap of ashes becomes his comforting place, an engulfing pit to hide. If you think at this point that Job has nothing to lose, I must tell you otherwise. In the depths of this darkness and "lostness," Job suddenly sees a ray of hope and a glimpse of Easter victory, and he sings the song of hope. "I know that my redeemer lives, and that in the end he will stand on the earth. And after my skin has been destroyed, yet in my flesh I will see God; I myself will see him with my own eyes—I, and not another" (Job 19:25–27). The word *redeemer* used in the Bible has been read for centuries by Christians to mean the One who came to redeem the world, the One and only mediator between man and God—Jesus the Christ. The prophet in Job looks forward to a future time, when that same One who was despised and rejected will rise again on Easter day. Job is talking about the power of resurrection. If Easter is true, the human race has hope for the future. The greatest declaration of the events that led up to Easter is a condition of hopelessness, and tragedies like an ash heap—an ash heap of despair and burned-out hopes. When someone can see the bright light of resurrection from among a heap of ashes, that hope becomes more significant.

Job realizes that his Redeemer is indeed God, He also has the assurance that God is on his side and when he will see God with his own eyes. In other words, this oldest book of the Bible points us to the experience of newness in resurrection. It is something like the experience of the disciples after resurrection, declaring that the race is not over. It only has started with resurrection. The resurrection experience is not about a coming world; rather, it is a reality here and now. The message from Job is that "in my flesh I will see God" (Job 19:26). I consider this a song of hope that Job wrote and sang when he thought about the renewal he awaited through resurrection of his body. The power of resurrection is an experience in our life in this world. The resurrection is about God's commitment to this world of flesh and blood. When you find yourself having lost fame, family, friends, health, and wealth; when your own spouse and servants despise and find you repulsive, there is a God who can and will redeem you and your situation. In the face of nothing, the promise of possessing everything. Be sure of the restoration God has planned for you, and God is on the side of the weak and vulnerable. Job experienced that beauty out of the ash heap just like the prophet who sang, "Bestow on them a crown of beauty instead of ashes, the oil of joy instead of mourning, and a garment of praise instead of a spirit of despair" (Isaiah 61:3).

Songs can bring comfort and company in the darkness of loneliness and grief of bereavement. Many saints have sung songs in the nights of their life that gave them the light in their paths. "When his lamp shone on my head and by his light I walked through darkness!" (Job 29:3). David says in Psalm 40:30 that he received a new song in his mouth. God promised the prophet Isaiah, "And you will sing as on the night you celebrate a holy festival; your hearts will rejoice as when people playing pipes go up to the mountain of the Lord, to the Rock of Israel" (Isaiah 30:29). If such songs are given to the pilgrims of the night, how joyfully shall they sing in that world where the sun shall set no more! "Weeping may stay for the night, but rejoicing comes in the morning" (Psalm 30:5). People of God wait for a time when there will be no more darkness. The Lord will light all the gloomy darkness. "There will be no more night. They will not need the light of a lamp or the light of the sun, for the Lord God will give them light. And they will reign for ever and ever" (Revelation 22:5).

CHAPTER 8

Radiance in Desolation

W hen we moved as a family to the United States in the early 1980s, things were not easy. We had our first baby during the first year in the United States. Since my wife was still in college, many plans that we had together were put on hold when we decided to focus on raising the baby. In addition to the family struggles, the conflicting values on cultural and moral struggles became real and stressful. It is difficult to sing in a foreign land when placed in a new culture and living conditions. To live out the witness as a Christian and keep the value as an Indian needed boldness. It is to be lived and spoken boldly, yet gently and respectfully.

The sons of Korah experienced this when they wrote the song "How can we sing the songs of the Lord while in a foreign land?" (Psalm 137:4). They hung their harps on the poplar trees near the Babylon River and wept thinking about their homeland. The psalm was written at a time they were in Babylonian exile that happened around 586 BC. Israel was conquered by the Babylonians in a terrible war. Many had been killed, and a lot were wounded. A lot of young men of talent were taken as captives and taken to Babylon. When the familiar has been ripped away from us, and we find ourselves in an unknown territory it is very difficult to sing songs even for the talented singers.

Sometimes life throws certain curveballs at us. The invasion of the world by the COVID-19 virus turned the world upside down into a state of desolation. Desolation means a state of bleak and dismal emptiness. Radiance on a person's face brings a ray of hope and purpose in such situations. Daniel's powerful example is one of courage combined with courtesy. Daniel prayed to God, "Lord, look with favor on your desolate sanctuary" (Daniel 9:17). Jesus said, "So when you see standing in the holy place 'the abomination that causes desolation, spoken of through the prophet Daniel—let the reader understand—then let those who are in Judea flee to the mountains" (Matthew 24:15–16). The "abomination of desolation" is mentioned three times in the book of Daniel (Daniel 9:27, 11:31, and 12:11).

The Jews are a group that were persecuted and scattered through history. The book of Daniel is full of stories about how many of them showed radiance on their faces in desolate circumstances. They were taken as slaves many times to Egypt, Babylon, Syria, and Rome. Over one million Jews were killed by Emperor Titus, who invaded in 70 AD. They were scattered all over the earth without a land to call their own. During the Second World War, under Hitler's holocaust, millions of Jews were tortured and killed. They finally founded their own country in 1948, and on their founding day, they were attacked on all their borders by the united forces of all the neighboring Muslim countries. Through it all, they bounced back, as the country of Israel now, raising their flag daily that carries the Star of David with greater radiance and brightness than ever, always holding on to their faith at the threat of their lives.

The four Hebrew boys in the book of Daniel knew firsthand the abomination in desolation. They were taken as captives to an idol-worshipping land, were given new home, new food, and new names. The natural response of people in such a situation would be to contest, complain, or give up. But these men chose a different path. They chose to shine brighter with radiance in the face of abomination. As Jesus said, they ran up to the mountains to rise above the situation and acted on a higher plane. They responded with gentleness and respect. They came up with newer options to keep their faith from compromise. Instead of making demands or refusing to eat the palace food, they asked for vegetables. They asked for a chance to test and prove their radiance with a lean diet. Their faces looked shinier and healthier than the people who feasted on the king's food.

The Hebrew men had a courageous faith that was also courteous. Many believers become arrogant and self-righteous. Bieng steadfast is like a thermostat that controls the environment, unlike a thermometer that moves up and down with the outside temperature. By His power, we can change the spiritual and moral temperature around us through a courageous and courteous faith. Our attitudes and responses bring warmth in cold situations. They bring cool air in the hot and burning situations of life. The four young men's faces shone with radiance after their test was over. They brought light and hope amid desolation and hopelessness. As Jesus said, rise to the mountaintop when you see desolation around you. As pilgrims climbed the mountain with singing and praising, we can rise to the mountaintop with songs of praises. Unlike in the valley, the mountaintop can give a higher vantage point and new perspectives. Christians ought to live on a higher plane than the world around them, rejoicing and praising God.

Faith is like a long-term investment; you don't trade it for short-term gains or enjoyment. In our walk of faith, we may be forced to take journeys to certain Babylon experiences—a faraway place in which you may feel uncomfortable and unpleasant. As children of God, we show the radiant light of the love of God to shine through the dark situation. The Babylonians could change their homes, their diet, their names, and their education, but they could never change their hearts and the radiance of their faith! They became agents of change in a godless and pagan land.

There was a birth of fear in the hearts of individuals like never before after the pandemic started. What is going to happen to our way of life and our freedoms? It is all about me! People of faith will need to think beyond themselves and step up and fight against situations like this with resolution and courage. The situation of uncertainty about the future has driven many into desolation and desperation. Studies are coming out about increased numbers of suicides, particularly among youngsters. In situations of desolation, faith brings our songs of praises to God. "So when you see standing in the holy place 'the abomination that causes desolation,' spoken of through the prophet Daniel—let the reader understand—then let those who are in Judea flee to the mountains" (Matthew 24:15–16).

Well-known singers sing not to make anyone sad, but to draw their sadness out of their souls to make room for joy to fill in. We don't want to cry and complain due to rage or hatred against anyone. We can cry in grief and sorrow with sweet songs on our lips that will make way for new hope, forgiveness, and love. Paul in his letter to the Thessalonians (4:13) encourages believers not to grieve without hope. We are faced with a strange situation due to the severity of the pandemic. Teachers are struggling how to teach, and parents are worried about the future of their children. Grandparents and relatives are now saying hi to each other online. The challenge here is to adapt and overcome by recognizing the situation as a reality and rising up to meet the challenge. Ultimately, the faith in an almighty God that led Israel will lead us too.

Corrie Ten Boom suffered at the hands of the Nazis in prison camps. Corrie suffered in the prison but would tell as many people as possible about the love and forgiveness of Jesus Christ every day in the camp. She obtained a small New Testament and smuggled it past guards, and her ministry began. She said, "Before long we were holding clandestine Bible study groups for an ever growing group of believers, and Barracks 28 became known throughout the camp as 'the wild place,' where they still hope." Corrie learned that the concentration camp was a place of hardship that also was a classroom of growth in God. Rise to the mountaintop when you see desolation around you. Unlike in the valley, on the mountaintop you can see a higher view. We are to live on a higher plane than the world around. Rise up and shine as radiant beams of hope amid confusion and desolation.

> Dare to be a Daniel, Dare to stand alone!
> Dare to have a purpose firm!
> Dare to make it known!
> Standing by a purpose true,
> Heeding God's command,
> Honor them, the faithful few! All hail
> to Daniel's band (Philip Bliss, 1873).

CHAPTER 9

Where Is God When
I Need Him?

I read the story of a frustrated mother whose two sons were driving her insane. She had tried everything to keep them in line. One day she had a discussion with a neighbor who said, "I took my son to our priest, and he got him straightened out." Because she didn't have a better idea, she followed her neighbor's advice and took her two sons to the local parish priest. The younger boy was left in the waiting room and the older boy was ushered into the presence of the priest.

Without so much as introducing himself, the priest stared into the eyes of the frightened boy and began his interrogation with this question: "Where is God?" The boy was speechless. The priest spoke again, "Where is God?" The boy looked away, searching the room as if the answer might be found in the religious items that filled the office. He still did not answer. A little louder and with more emphasis, the priest asked for a third time, "Where is God?"

This time, the boy leaped to his feet and ran out of the office. When he came to the waiting room, he grabbed his brother by the hand and pulled him out the door. "Let's get out of here," he said. "They've lost God and they're trying to pin it on us."

One time a man told me his experience of how he felt abandoned and lonely after his wife's death. He felt as though God was silent. The visits from his children added to his pain of loneliness when they left. He said he thought even God had abandoned him. God is nowhere near, and God had moved away and didn't leave a forwarding address!

The Bible is full of stories of people who said God seemed to be distant in certain times of their lives. David wrote a number of psalms, including Psalm 13 when he thought God was away. "How long, Lord? Will you forget me forever?" (Psalm 13:1). In Psalm 42:3 the psalmist asks, "My tears have been my food day and night, while people say to me all day long, "Where is your God?" Asaph asks in Psalm 79:10: "Why should the nations say, "Where is their God?" In Job 35:9, Elihu, a friend of Job asks: "No one says, 'Where is God my Maker, who gives songs in the night?" Understanding God's silence is not easy because our natural tendency is to interpret the silence as indifference.

In the gospel according to John chapter 11, we read about Jesus raising a man named Lazarus from death. Mary and Martha were facing the heartache of the sickness of their brother Lazarus and then his death. They sent for Jesus, but He stayed where He was for another couple of days. They might have asked the same question as to why Jesus did not show up sooner. Jesus, the Son of God, cried on the cross with agonizing pain of suffering for the sins of the world, "My God, my God, why have you forsaken me?" (Matthew 27:46). These are all valid biblical questions a believer might ask. The Jews, schooled in the Old Testament, and like almost all other religions, would say: "Where God is, there is no misery." We tend to think on the positive side of faith to believe that all is well when we have faith. But Jesus came to this world to turn that upside down. We can change that saying to, "Where there is misery, there is God." Jesus voluntarily embraced misery to share the pain and suffering with us. In other words, as an author puts it, "Where misery is, there is the Messiah."

Philip Yancey while talking to the Virginia Tech students in June 2007 in a sermon given on the school campus two weeks after the mass shooting said, "Why do bad things happen? I cannot tell you, and I encourage you to resist anyone who offers a confident answer. God himself did not answer that question for Job, nor did Jesus answer the why questions. We have hints, but no one knows the full answer. What we do know, with full confidence, is how God feels. We know how God looks on a broken world, and gave us Jesus, a face that was streaked with tears, that felt the suffering with us."

Frederick Buechner, a theologian and a minister, said, "I am not the Almighty God, but if I were, maybe, I would out of mercy heal the pain of the world in a second or out of mercy, kick the world to pieces in its pain." But God did neither. He sent Jesus. God joined our world in all its unutterable pain. He loves you with an everlasting and tender love, and He is grieved by your pain. He wants to share your burdens and pains with you. He wants you to give Him all the circumstances that have hurt you. When you do, He will be able to release you from the pain you are carrying. God is in the business of redeeming what is broken when we feel like God is far away.

Nobody can promise that there will be no pain or suffering. But we can stand behind the promise that the apostle Paul made in Romans 8 that all things can be redeemed and can work together for your good. In another passage, Paul spells out some of the things he encountered, which included beatings, imprisonment, and shipwreck. As he looked back, he could see that somehow God had redeemed even those crisis events in his life. Paul concluded. "In all these things we are more than conquerors through him who loved us. For I am convinced that neither death nor life, neither angels nor demons, neither the present nor the future, nor any powers, neither height nor depth, nor anything else in all creation, will be able to separate us from the love of God that is in Christ Jesus our Lord" (Romans 8:37–39). God's love is reigning over us as the foundational truth of the universe. That is good reason to sing praises to God.

Where is God when it hurts? That becomes a personal question to each of us. Each of us is part of the body of Christ wherever we are placed in life. We become the presence and the hands of God wherever we are. The church is the body while

Christ is the head. We are all faced with a question that needs an answer from each of us at some point. Instead of asking, "Where is God when it hurts?" as followers of Christ, we need to rise up above the hurt and ask the question, "Where is the church when it hurts?"

In the March 2010 issue of *Our Daily Bread* devotional, there is a story of a single mother by name Leslie who had been behind in her mortgage payment due to unemployment. She and her two daughters were about to be evicted from their home. Although Leslie believed that God could help, so far He hadn't given a clue as to how. As she drove to the courthouse, she prayed for God's intervention. Then she heard a song on the radio proclaiming, "God is here! Let the brokenhearted rejoice." Could this be the assurance from God that she was longing to hear? Inside the courtroom, Leslie stood before the judge with tearful eyes and a heavy heart. She heard the court's decision and signed the legal documents to give away her home to the bank; still, God had not given her an answer. Leslie was walking out of the courtroom with her two little girls, not knowing when they would be kicked out of their house, and she did not know where to go. She wondered, *Where is God when I need Him?* Still, she held on to a small ray of faith and refused to see God as a silent witness to her trouble.

As Leslie was walking in the parking lot of the court to her car, a truck pulled up beside her. "Ma'am," said the driver, "I heard your testimony inside the courtroom, and I believe God wants me to help you." And he did. Gary was in the courtroom for another matter. He helped Leslie get in contact with a woman from his local church who was able to work with the parties involved to reverse the process so that she and her girls could stay in their home.

Yes, Leslie has an answer to all those who ask, "Where is God when it hurts?" The answer is, "Right here, where we are." Yes, we know where God is. He is in our midst. With their experience and testimony of life full with the faithfulness of God, believers will answer the question, "Yes, God is here in our midst." He is the "Emmanuel," God with us, in joy or pain, in grief or sorrow, on the mountaintop or in the valley. Yes, He is with us. That is the song of rejoicing when God fills the voids in our lives.

God is with us in the suffering because He loves us. "God demonstrates His own love toward us, in that while we were still sinners, Christ died for us" (Romans 5:8). Our relationship with God is not based on our merits but is based on the grace and love of God. God loves us beyond measure. God loves each one of us as if you were the only one to love. He so loved us that He gave His only Son to die for us. In grief, love and pain converge. In Jesus, God joined us and shared our human condition, including its great grief. The foundation of our faith is that God is love. To love means to feel pain and to grieve. Pain is a mark of life. In the walk of Jesus, we see Jesus joining the people and families in their grief and pain. Jesus is seen weeping with them as He did at the death of His friend Lazarus. God so loved the world that He sent His only son unconditionally to die for us. Hebrews 2:9 reads: "But we do see Jesus, who was made lower than the angels for a little while, now crowned with glory and honor because he suffered death, so that by the grace of God he might taste death for everyone."

God is not punishing us for our mistakes through our hurts because He is a good God. His goodness will not change based on our actions or reactions. "He does not treat us as our sins deserve or repay us according to our iniquities" (Psalm 103:10). Amid pain, it is hard to see the good. It is easy to question God: "Why did God let this happen? Why me?" No human can answer these questions.

Job is a famous man in the Old Testament, and he suffered about as much as anyone you'd ever want to meet. He had several friends visit him for days and talk to him to find answers for him about the tragedy. He calls those who tried to find answers to his problems "miserable comforters" (Job 16:2), the ones who tried to find answers to his sickness, "worthless physicians" (Job 13:4), and maxims like "proverbs of ashes" (Job 13:12). Job was a blameless and upright man. Job knew God was not punishing him. He trusted a God who is the source of all comfort, healer of all sicknesses, and the Living Word that continues to comfort.

CHAPTER 10

Puzzle Pieces

Is life a work of art or a puzzle? Life can be a puzzle. Some get the prizes they never expected, and some are surprised. Life can be a puzzle that when put together becomes a beautiful work of art. What is the most exciting time in the process of solving a puzzle? The beginning? Or as we get each piece? Or is it at the end when all pieces are complete? When does a song become a song? While it written or while it is sung?

We all have different lives and different ends. A preacher and the church bus driver were standing at the entrance to heaven. The guard who checks in welcomed the bus driver and said, "Welcome, I am in charge of housing. I understand that you were a bus driver. You are being assigned that great mansion over the hill." The preacher, who was watching and hearing this, thought to himself, "If the bus driver got a beautiful mansion,

I must get a beautiful palace." As the preacher was checking in, the guard said, "I am in charge of housing and see that you worked as a preacher. You are assigned that cabin in the terrace under that mansion." The preacher protested. "I worked as a pastor helping people to come to God; I worked hard and made a lot of sacrifices. It is not fair that the bus driver gets a mansion, and I get a little cabin." The guard said, "It seems that when you preached, people were sleeping. But when the driver was driving, people were praying." (https://davesgarden.com/community/forums/t/1425366/#b)

When our boys were young, they were thrilled by jigsaw puzzles. When they were in a store and saw a new jigsaw puzzle, one of them used to make his choice based on the picture on the outside of the box, and the other picked up based on the difficulty. Yes, it is true in life. Some get to solve the easy puzzles, while others seem to face the challenging ones. But in either case, the potential beauty that it can become is rewarding. However, when we first open the box, the puzzle looks nothing like the picture on the outside; it is simply jumbled pieces in a bag.

If life is compared to a puzzle, it may be a simple puzzle with a hundred different pieces, or it may be a more complicated thousand-piece puzzle with a picture that is rather tricky to put together. There may be unpleasant and uncomfortable pieces in life that you feel like not fitting in. You have been able to put together everything well for years but all of a sudden find yourself confused as to how to fit in the next event. But whatever the size of the challenge, those events can be gifts.

In the book of Genesis, we read the story of Joseph, who was treated harshly and eventually sold to foreigners by his own brothers. He went on to become the ruler of the foreign land. When the other brothers were reunited with Joseph after several years, they were afraid that the powerful Joseph would retaliate. But he replied to his brothers, "Don't be afraid. Am I in the place of God? You intended to harm me, but God intended it for good to accomplish what is now being done, the saving of many lives. So then, don't be afraid. I will provide for you and your children." And he reassured them and spoke kindly to them." (Genesis 50:20–21).

Joseph's life was one filled with wrongful accusations and betrayals. He was betrayed by his brothers, falsely accused by his master's wife, and thrown into prison and left to languish there for years. Yet when Joseph surveyed his circumstances, he was able to proclaim with boldness that what others meant for evil, God had used for good. The torn robe became a royal one, and the pit became a palace. The broken family grew older and came back together. The very acts intended to destroy God's servant turned out to strengthen him. We all face the kinds of struggles that can leave us puzzled by worry, anger, or sadness. We may feel broken, like the puzzle pieces in the bag. But God can always see the bigger picture—the picture on the outside of the box.

Many fail to pay close attention to the bigger picture on the outside of the box. A man approached a laborer who was laying bricks and asked him, "What are you doing?" The laborer said, "Can't you see I'm laying bricks?" The man then walked over to another bricklayer and asked, "What are you doing?" And the workman answered with pride, "I'm building a palace." Both were physically doing the same thing, but the first laborer was occupied with the present task, and the other was concerned with the ultimate goal. Trust in God that our lives were made with a purpose. A life without purpose is like a race without a finish line. Let us run that race with a goal to finish.

In the "big picture," we all have something meaningful to add, and we all have our rightful place in the grand design of the Creator. "He has made everything beautiful in its time. He has also set eternity in the human heart; yet no one can fathom what God has done from beginning to end" (Ecclesiastes 3:11). Although the burdens of life will arise, God takes the broken pieces of our pain, sadness, worry, and grief and works in them to create something beautiful and whole. God knows the potential we hold. When our hearts are heavy and our strength is low, we can trust that with God, our puzzles will be completed for a beauty at last.

We build our lives just as you would a puzzle—piece by piece and section by section. You may get bored at times, or frustrated, or feel as though you'd rather give up. What you must do, however, is know that the pieces are all there, and the more ways you try to place them where they belong, the more connections you discover. Soon you begin to visualize and discern images as they come together to form the overall vision of your life. You will see a beautiful work of art unfolded eventually. Socrates said, "The world is a puzzle; no need to make sense out of it." But we want to make sense of our lives because we live only once. We cannot understand everything, but we certainly want our lives to have meaning and purpose.

As my wife and I were walking in the trail one day, we noticed a large abnormal growth on a tree about the size of a volleyball. This was caused by a type of cancer that makes the cells grow out of control. The cells of that limb grow in many different shapes and patterns. It looked ugly and deformed in our eyes. But when we talked to a friend who is an expert in trees, he said that such growths are invaluable to wood carving experts. They can make beautiful carvings with multicolored swirls and waves using such pieces. They polish it to make it a beautiful work of art. Similarly, our loving God is the skilled artist who can turn our deformed situations and brokenness into unique and beautiful works of art adorned with grace and love.

Mary was not a leprosy patient. Rather, she worked as a medical resident at Brand's leprosy hospital in India. One day she went on a picnic outing in a vehicle driven by a young student. Their vehicle was faced with a head-on collision with another car. Their car veered over a bridge and tumbled down a steep embankment. Mary Verghese, a promising young physician, lay motionless at the bottom of the bank. Her face was badly injured and deformed. She lost sensitivity and motion below the waist. Mary's next few months were almost unbearable. As summer temperatures reached 110 degrees outside, Mary lay in her sweltering hospital room, in traction, wrapped in a thick jacket and plastic brace. She faced agonizing hours of therapy.

Each week nurses would test her for sensation, and each week she would fail, never feeling the pinpricks on her legs.

After observing her downward spiral of despair, Dr. Brand stopped by her room for a visit. "Mary," he began, "I think it's time to begin thinking of your professional future as a doctor." At first she thought he was joking, but he went on to suggest that she might bring to other patients unique qualities of sympathy and understanding. She pondered his suggestion a long time, doubting whether she would ever recover sufficient use of her limbs to function as a doctor.

Gradually, Mary, on a wheelchair, began to work with the leprosy patients. The hospital staff noticed that the patients' self-pity, hopelessness, and sullenness seemed to fade when Mary Verghese was around. Leprosy patients whispered among themselves about the wheelchair doctor (the first in India) who was more disabled than they were, whose face, like theirs, bore scars. Before long Mary Verghese began assisting at surgery—tedious, exhausting work for her in a sitting position. One day Dr. Brand met Mary rolling her wheelchair between buildings of the hospital and asked how she was doing. "At first the threads seemed so tangled and broken," she replied, "but I'm beginning to think life may have a pattern after all." Mary's recovery was to involve many excruciating hours of therapy, as well as major surgery on her spine. She remained incontinent for life and fought constantly against pressure sores. But she now had a glimmer of hope. She began to understand that the disability was not a punishment sent by God to entrap her in a life of misery. Rather, it could be transformed into her greatest asset as a doctor. In her wheelchair, with her crooked smile, she had immediate rapport with disabled patients. Eventually, Mary learned to walk with braces. She worked under scholarship in New York's Institute of Physical Medicine and Rehabilitation and ultimately headed up a new department at the Physiotherapy School in Vellore, India.

Mary stands as an outstanding example of a person who got nowhere asking why a tragedy happened. But as she turned toward God and asked to what end, she learned to trust Him to weave a new design for her life. In doing so, Mary Verghese has probably achieved far more than she would have had the accident not occurred. (Mary's story is told in "Take My Hands" by Dorothy Clarke Wilson.)

Moses, Abraham, David, Joseph, and many others stand as examples of how puzzle pieces of life come together to make a masterpiece. The finished masterpiece is a memory forever that gives us the greatest satisfaction. Just like the sweetest songs are sometimes those that are composed with the saddest notes of life, the most beautiful picture comes out of the hardest puzzle pieces of life.

One thing I wouldn't do after finishing a jigsaw puzzle was to take it apart and do it again. Instead, I would either leave it on a table with a cardboard background, or I would glue the pieces together with a special glue and hang the finished masterpiece up on a wall for all to see. The same thing is true for everyone. Life is truly a masterpiece. The only difference here between your life and the jigsaw puzzle is that life is not a finished work yet. Because your life is always evolving, it is always changing.

But what does stay the same is that every trait that makes up your magnificent being is always there. It just changes its form over time.

Always seek the best possible outcome. Concern yourself with what you can control. Look for the lesson to be gleaned, not what you may lose. Remember the wise words passed down from people who knew: This too shall pass! So, above all things, be patient and make the most out of every moment. Our prayer must be that God may work in the struggles of our lives to help us turn them into songs of testimonies of resilience and strength. That is when people of faith can sing joyous songs of celebrations.

CHAPTER 11

A Time for Everything

66 There is a time for everything, and a season for every activity under the heavens" (Ecclesiastes 3:1). In the 1960s a rock band in the United States named the Byrds popularized this verse with their song "Turn! Turn! Turn!" In 1965, however, they emphasized the "time of peace" at the end, turning these verses into a plea for world calm. John Grisham's first novel, *A Time to Kill*, also takes its title from this verse.

Welcoming a new year is a time when we reflect on our lives and make plans for the future. A common excuse we hear for failure to do is, "I didn't have time." It happens every year. Most of us check our watch several times a day—or several times an hour. Sometimes we do it more often than we should, like when we're in church because we know time goes by very fast. We are all constantly aware of time. We have a time to get up, to eat, to go to work, to go to gym, and to go to bed. You and I probably have a dozen clocks and four or five calendars in our homes. It is about time to think about time. Solomon is not just talking about the value of time, but also the timing of events in this universe. The events of our lives do not randomly happen by chance; God has a purpose behind them.

Some in our family got the same gifts at Christmas one time from a particular person. It was a wellness keeper, an interesting technical device known as Fitbit. These are activity trackers, wireless-enabled wearable technology devices that measure data such as the number of steps walked, heart rate, quality of sleep, steps climbed, and other personal metrics involved in fitness. Recently, a person showed me that the reason she was not performing well at work was due to bad quality sleep. She pointed to her Fitbit as the proof. Users can log their food, activities, and weight, to track over time, and can set daily and weekly goals for themselves for steps, calories burned and consumed, and distance walked. Calories in versus calories out is more accurately measured when app users keep their tracker on. There was no evidence that the devices altered the amount that people exercised or their diet compared to control. Well, people still spend money on this.

All users had the option to make their physical activity information private, but some users were unaware that the information was public by default. One specific issue, which technology blogs made fun of, was that some users were including details about their private lives in their daily exercise logs, and this information was, by default, publicly available.

Fitbit responded to criticism by making all such data private by default and requesting that search engines remove indexed user profile pages from their databases. The company's devices have also been used in criminal investigations; in one instance, a rape claim against an unnamed intruder was turned around to a criminal charge for false reports based on data from the claimant's Fitbit. Fitbit has helped solve murders and crimes.

One thing all of these technologies prove is that "time" goes by while you plan on the things you want to do. Time is an equal opportunity provider. Every person gets the same amount of time every day—–24 hours. Sometimes it seems to fly away; sometimes it seems to drag. To be brutally honest, we waste a lot of time, knowingly or unknowingly. We can and should be creative with the usage of time. Paul says, "Be very careful, then, how you live—not as unwise but as wise, making the most of every opportunity, because the days are evil" (Ephesians 5:15–16).

The author of Ecclesiastes, believed to be Solomon, illustrates this truth by comparing the opposites: fourteen pairs of contrasting activities as examples of how life is comprised of various seasons. A straightforward reading of the passage reveals that there are good and bad events listed. He is not justifying one over the other, rather states that God's plan for life involves a variety of experiences and activities. Weeping may be part of life, but life is not all weeping; laughter has a place too (Ecclesiastes 3:4). Construction is good in its time, but sometimes deconstruction is unavoidable. Wars may not be good, but they become a reality at times.

The word translated "time" means "can be considered a point in time." There are seasons in time, and there are points in time. Within any given season, there is a point in time in which God has ordained everything to happen. So, season means a period of time, and time means a point in time. In weather, there are seasons. Thank God for the seasons because all sunshine and no rain make a desert. Nature has a season of growth, but within that season there is a time to plant and a time to harvest. Sowing first, then, after a season or duration, there is harvesting. In life, there are dozens of different seasons. "A time to be born and a time to die, a time to plant and a time to uproot" (Ecclesiastes 3:2). Every season of life includes both good and bad times. We go through mountains, and we go through valleys. We go through successes, and we go through failures. We have wins, and we have losses. Life is a combination of contrasting seasons.

There's also the process of constructing and destroying, or tearing down. A building is built in a few months, and then, fifty years or so later, that building is torn down. The destruction of the building is usually faster than its construction, but the duration of usage (season) is most of the time longer than either the time of building or the time of tearing down. It may take two years to build a structure, but we use it for years before tearing down. Verse 5 says, "A time to scatter stones and a time to gather them" (Ecclesiastes 3:5). Again, using the image of building, there's a time to cast away the stones from your fields so that you can farm the fields. And then there's a time to pick up those stones on the edge of the field and build a house with them. Our life seasons are about building and rebuilding.

Verse 6 continues this thought: "a time to search and a time to give up, a time to keep and a time to throw away" (Ecclesiastes 3:6). There is a time to go shopping (the time some like best) and a time to throw old, useless things away (the time some hate the most). But many do not have the same disposition when it comes time to part with those things. After the season of usefulness, the time to gain is over, and the time to throw away has come. The invention of garage sale has somewhat reduced the pain of this parting. There is duration—a season of time—for everything, and then there is a point in time for change.

We read here that there is "a time to love and a time to hate, a time for war and a time for peace" (Ecclesiastes 3:8). Of course, Solomon is not advocating either hate or war. But the reality is, there are things for us to hate (the things God hates), and there may be a time for us to fight battles. His point is that we are to balance all the times of our lives so that the season pleases God. If things do not go your way, give it time. If things are going your way, use those times for the preparation for time when they won't. Set your sights on the duration season, not on the peaks and valleys of time. Build your life on God's Word, and you will be a seasoned Christian. Build your life on the things that happen in time, and you will be an unhappy Christian.

Everyone goes through good times and bad times; together they make up the season of life. It's not the times of our lives that shape us but the seasons. We cannot live only for the good times; when the bad times come (and they will), we should be able to handle them. And make sure you don't let the bad times defeat you. If you do, you'll miss out on all the good times God still has in store for you. It takes both to make a life. The key is that even if you can't enjoy all the times, you do enjoy the season. Praise God that neither good times nor bad times last; only eternity does.

There is beauty in time. "He has made everything beautiful in its time" (Ecclesiastes 3:11). The proper event at the right time that brings about God's purposes is a beautiful part of the overall plan. Each day is a gift from the hand of God. Ecclesiastes 3:1–8 explains it is because God has a reason and a time for all things. People may be ignorant of God's timing (Ecclesiastes 3:9–11), but they are called to enjoy life in the present (3:12–13) and trust in God's sovereignty (3:14–15). The reality of life is that everything is not beautiful. Cancer is not beautiful. Child abuse is not beautiful. War is not beautiful. Ecclesiastes 3:11 can be read as God has made everything beautiful for its own time. That's very different from everything is beautiful in its own way. God can take even the bad things and, in the proper season, turn them around and use them for good in the way He intends. Accordingly, God will never be late, and He will never be early. Furthermore, He knows the proper duration for that event. He never holds it over too long or cuts it off too short.

You may be going through a season right now that is not beautiful. Your finances may look ugly. Your health may look not so beautiful. Your marriage or a relationship may look ugly.

Your future may look troublesome. If you believe that nothing happens by chance, and the events that occur are not just random happenings determined by the roll of dice, then they happen in accordance with the will of our Creator (Romans 8:28). For example, Solomon outlines fourteen opposite activities to demonstrate that there is a proper time for all human activity. At the appropriate point in time, God will make everything fit into the season of your life. It is like the pieces of a puzzle. You struggle to piece things together, and then suddenly things just seem to fall into place. That's what happens when you commit both your times and your seasons to God.

The word translated "beautiful" means more like "fitting," or "appropriate." There is a fitting point in time that God has determined something should happen. In the same fashion, God knows the most fitting points and the most appropriate seasons of our lives as well. He knows exactly the number of days of your life. Nobody can change the length of a person's life. Our times and seasons are in God's hand. He is the Creator who makes "proper" in its time whatever we entrust in His hands.

The most beautiful thing God has created is you and me. At the right time of God, you were born; each event is timed in the plan of God for you. *The Upper Room* devotional wrote a story about a bus called "Special" that was used to take Honduran villagers to church. Even though it had a cracked windshield along with mechanical problems, it was used for an important purpose. Then I thought about some of the people that I know—people who are less than perfect. I thought of Joseph, the driver who lost his finger but who can drive the bus; of the old evangelist whom some people regard as strange but who shares his life stories; and of the boy with Down's syndrome who seems to know when someone is suffering and offers them hugs, even though his words are difficult to understand. None of us is perfect. But just as God uses the bus called Special and people regarded as strange or disabled by human standards, God can use us for divine purposes. Broken buses, people with mental or physical disabilities—God calls each of us to special service in this world.

Whether you've just walked through the greatest year of your life or are incredibly glad to see this one finally over, one thing is certain: God excels in making all things new. God makes everything beautiful. And although a fresh calendar year or an anniversary can never erase all the struggles or pain you may have faced this past year, God has the power to work through even the hardest of times, bringing renewed purpose, greater strength, and a hope that the world cannot ever offer.

Perhaps you are getting married or becoming a parent for the first time. Maybe you are leaving school and entering the workforce or moving from full-time work to retirement. As we move from season to season, our priorities change. We may need to put aside what we did in the past and funnel our energy into something else. When life brings changes in our circumstances and obligations, we must responsibly and wisely discern what kind of commitments we should make, seeking in whatever we do to "do it all for the glory of God" (1 Corinthians 10:31). As we acknowledge Him in all our ways, He will guide us in the way we should go. The loving heavenly Father will give us wisdom to know what priorities we need to have at this season of our life. Paul says, "And do this, understanding the present time: The hour has already come for you to wake up from your slumber, because our salvation is nearer now than when we first believed. The night is nearly over; the day is almost here. So let us put aside the deeds of darkness and put on the armor of light" (Romans 13:11–12).

After Jacob had seen his long-lost son, Joseph, he said, "Now I am ready to die, since I have seen for myself that you are still alive" (Genesis 46:30). He knew his days had been fulfilled. The duration—the season—was fulfilled. The exact day of his death was in God's hands. But Jacob knew this season of his life had reached its completion. In a world of heroic medical care and wonder drugs, let us not forget that just as the day of our birth was part of God's eternal timetable, so is the day of our death. None of us likes the idea of facing death, but those who have trusted Jesus Christ as Savior can face it very differently than those who are fearing the consequences of their sin. For believers, the day of our death is another day to glorify the Lord. The day when we die is simply another day to commit to a loving and omniscient God. The day of our death is in His hands every bit as wonderful as the day of our birth. "The Lord has done it this very day; let us rejoice today and be glad" (Psalm 118:24).

You may have gone through rejection or abandonment, but the promise of God's word for the future is alive. There is an answer. The answer is God has a plan for your life. It is through faith in Jesus Christ as your Savior that God can make your life beautiful, and He does it in His own time. And maybe this is God's time for you. Let Him make your life beautiful. "For I know the plans I have for you," declares the Lord, "plans to prosper you and not to harm you, plans to give you hope and a future." (Jeremiah 29:11).

My friend Billy said, "I was a revolutionary when I decided to join seminary and my prayer to God was: 'Lord, with your help, I am here to change the world.'" As he approached the end of the seminary life, his prayer became: "Lord, give me the grace to change all those who come into contact with me, my family, and friends. I shall be satisfied." When he was toward the end of his life, he said his prayer changed to: "Lord, give me the grace to change myself." If he had prayed for this right from the start, he would have been more satisfied.

Time as we describe and understand now is comparatively new. From a railroad engineer's suggestions, time was finally standardized in the United States on November 18, 1883. Before that, every community decided what time it was on their own. All railroads out of New York ran on New York time, and railroads west from Chicago mostly used Chicago time, but between Chicago and Pittsburgh/Buffalo the norm was Columbus time. Standard time was not enacted into US law until the 1918 Standard Time Act established standard time in time zones; the law also instituted daylight saving time (DST). Back in 1792, the French tried a ten-day week with ten hours in a day, 100 minutes in an hour and 100 seconds in a minute. The Russians tried a five-day week in 1929 and even named the days of the week after colors. Although the way we describe time hasn't been around all that long, God has been working with time since the beginning of creation. In fact, He's the originator of time. The first mention of time is in Genesis 1:5: "So the evening and the morning were the first day."

Our knowledge of time is very limited. We don't know where it came from and where it is going. But one thing we all know—our time in this world is limited. So, we must make the best use of the time. Mark Twain said, "Twenty years from now you will be more disappointed by the things that you didn't do than by the ones you did do. So, throw off the bowlines. Sail away from the safe harbor. Catch the trade winds in your sails. Explore. Dream. Discover." Then you can sing joyfully the "song of time."

CHAPTER 12

Cakes Not Turned

My wife loves to cook. She follows anything out there online and will try to make things that are delicious and tasty. One time she taught a cooking class in a group to show how to make chicken fried rice. She does not use ounce cups or spoons, because most often she can guess by using her judgment. One of the attendees asked her about how much salt she added. She replied, "This much" by pouring some salt into her palm. They all looked at each other and laughed. We don't have to be perfect or experts to use our skills. We all have skills and talents that we can use if we are willing to step up and use opportunities available all around.

Our life is a pursuit of perfection. We don't need to be perfect in anything but to show the world that we are still a work in progress. The prophet Hosea was a contemporary with

Isaiah and Micah, whose career spanned over a period of sixty years during the times of the last six kings of the northern kingdom. God called Hosea to prophesy during Israel's last hours as a nation. God would call Jeremiah to do the same type of ministry in the southern kingdom of Judah. The book of Hosea can be considered as God's last gracious effort to stop the decline of the kingdom. Though Israel had given up on God, they are still not abandoned by God. According to the prophet, "Ephraim is a flat loaf not turned over" (Hosea 7:8). A pancake not cooked on both sides is not good for anything.

I am not into cooking due to the disastrous results of burning and flaming that had led to many dangerous situations. The sort of cake to which Ephraim is here likened is something like a pancake they call "Uggah," which literally means "circular." A scorching heat was applied on one side; sometimes by means of hot charcoal heaped upon it; sometimes (it is thought) the fire was within the earthen jar, around which the thin dough was fitted. Using this metaphor, Hosea warns the people for their insincerity and ingratitude to God. He says that they are like the cake that was cooked on one side but not turned. One side is burned while the other is not cooked. It needs to be turned for the other side to cook properly. In fact, a cake burnt on one side and unbaked on the other is inedible, which shows an image of the worthlessness.

The people of Israel considered themselves to be consecrated people of God, but they were worshipping idols and living a life of sin. Their theology was "half-baked," which makes it useless as a food for the soul. A Christian may be "well done" externally but raw and uncooked on the inside. Nonetheless, the prophet punctuates his message with a consolation and hope for the future. "His splendor will be like an olive tree, his fragrance like a cedar of Lebanon. People will dwell again in his shade" (Hosea 14:6).

Jesus said, "Woe to you, teachers of the law and Pharisees, you hypocrites! You clean the outside of the cup and dish, but inside they are full of greed and self-indulgence. Blind Pharisee! First clean the inside of the cup and dish, and then the outside also will be clean" (Matthew 23:25–28). They are ready to serve and worship on the outside, while their inside is full of hypocrisy and lawlessness. A Christian may be "well done" on Sunday morning but raw and rough during the rest of the week. Jesus continued to say, "What goes into someone's mouth does not defile them, but what comes out of their mouth, that is what defiles them" (Matthew 15:11).

Modern religion does not like the word *sin* or calling anyone a sinner. The society likes to promote positive attitude, which is good in many cases, but not when it comes to teaching about sin. Having a positive attitude is very good and advisable. At the same time, we should be aware of the negative forces that can impact our success as individuals. Sin is often not addressed by the word *sin*. Some may like to call it "weakness, mistake, or shortcoming." No matter what we call it, they point to the same nature that produces results that are destructive and pervasive. You can label a bottle full of sugar with the label "pepper." But an ant knows it is sugar and still finds its way to it. We are all sinful by nature, sinning against one another and against God. Sin has consequences. Sin tears us down physically, emotionally, and spiritually. It gives more trouble over time. "Can a man scoop fire into his lap without his clothes being burned? Can a man walk on hot coals without his feet being scorched?" (Proverbs 6:27–29). It affects our body—like addictions and health issues. David's sin began to take a physical toll on him, and he said, "Let the bones you have crushed rejoice" (Psalm 51:8).

Dangers of sin can be compared to the dangers of radioactivity. Madame Marie Curie holds her place in history as a pioneer in the study of radioactivity. In 1903, she was the first woman to win the Nobel Prize, capturing the honor in physics. Then, in 1911, she received a second Nobel Prize, this one in chemistry. Such a wonderful contribution did not come without tremendous sacrifice. Madame Curie died of leukemia caused by prolonged exposure to radioactive materials. Even today, scholars who wish to read her handwritten journals and lab papers must wear protective clothing because these archives are still radioactive. Sinful behaviors and action can produce lasting consequences in our body and may be transferred to generations. "Trouble pursues the sinner" (Proverbs 13:21).

Sin affects our mind and our relationships with one another. Sin will become very personal to the deepest core of the soul. Sin will tell you, "You can get by with it!" or "No one will ever know about it!" Then, after you do it, sin says, "You'll never get away with it, everyone is going to find out!" The force of guilt empowers the mind. Sin pulls the sinner down, then convinces them that they will never be able to get back up again. It frustrates and throw us into depression and death.

Sin inflicts two major wounds to the mind—guilt and sorrow. Sorrow may heal. Guilt festers and infects the whole of life, until it is dealt with. It manifests itself in our temper, lack of concentration, irritability, no prayer life, lack of appetite for spiritual things, etc.

Sin affects our spirit and our relationship with God. David acknowledges in Psalm 51:4 that the sin he committed was against God. He asks God to restore the joy of salvation that he lost to sin. David was broken because he had hurt God! His joy had been lost because he had hurt his heavenly Father. Sin will make you the most miserable person on the face of the earth. A true Christian weeps not over the consequences of his actions; he weeps because he has offended and disgraced his heavenly Father! When we are burdened with sin, we get a kind of "spiritual indigestion." We become critical, sour, and judgmental, impossible to satisfy and quick to attack others to make ourselves look better. We feel so miserable and attempt to compensate by pushing the pain off on others.

Human sin is so terrible that it cannot be cured through moral and religious laws. The Bible teaches that the wages of sin is death and can only be appropriated by the death of a sinless man. Sin necessitated the death of a sinless savior. Jesus, who was God, became man and died for our sins and was raised for our justification. "He was delivered over to death for our sins and was raised to life for our justification" (Romans 4:25). You cannot be saved by your good works, because no matter how hard you try, your "good" is not good enough for the perfectly holy and completely righteous God who alone grants salvation.

Isaiah 64:6 says all our good works are like filthy rags. Paul teaches that "we are dead in our sins" (Ephesians 2:1). A dead person can do nothing but lie there and be dead and helpless. But the good news is that all are justified freely by His grace through the redemption that came by Christ Jesus. Second Corinthians 5:21 says it well: "God made him who had no sin to be sin for us, so that in him we might become the righteousness of God." We can be restored and made whole. We can get back the joy once lost. Even the most holy saints will sin, but the difference from a nonbeliever is that the saint will repent and seek forgiveness from God and from those who are affected by it.

Conviction makes us sad; confession makes us glad. Sin seals the lips, but repentance and forgiveness make us joyful where one will start singing the songs of salvation and deliverance. Once your sins are forgiven, God sees you not as you are but as who you can become. We read about the encounter of a short and mean tax collector and Jesus. Because of his short stature, he had to climb upon a tree to see Jesus in the crowd. Everyone else looked at Zacchaeus and saw a mean, little, dirty, rotten sinner. When Jesus looked at him on that tree, He did not see a crooked tax collector; He saw a man who could become a child of God. He saw a man who could be so generous he would give half of his money away. At the tree, Jesus did not tell him to repent and pay back to those people from whom he took money illegally and then he would be glad to visit him. Instead, Jesus said, "Zacchaeus, come down immediately. I must stay at your house today" (Luke 19:5).

"If we confess our sins, he is faithful and just and will forgive us our sins and purify us from all unrighteousness" (1 John 1:9). Jesus says the same to you today. You may have made mistakes. Jesus is here today to lovingly call you by name and invite you to become friends with Him. Unlike a cake that is not turned, He wants us to become useful in His hands as a well cooked and turned cake.

CHAPTER 13

Treasure in Clay Pots

It is reason to sing joyfully when you realize how feeble and delicate our lives are and how the almighty God protects us. Like a mother bird protects the chicks from harm, God protects us from the storms of life. Our lives are very tender like clay pots, which can be easily broken by even the smallest hurts. Even when broken, God can use the broken pieces to produce something better or even beautiful. As we see the pandemic take away the lives of thousands around us, it is not anybody's merit that counts who are alive, but it is just the grace of God.

Alexis Leon was working as a technical consultant in Chennai, India. December 2, 1993, started as a regular day in his life. This time was one of the happiest periods of his life. He was going to get married on December 26. He had just gotten a promotion and new assignment, and was going to Switzerland in January, where he planned to spend the honeymoon. Everything seemed fine and perfect.

By around 11:00 a.m., he left the office for an appointment on his motorcycle. He was crossing the road in front of his office at an intersection, when another vehicle ran the red light at very high speed and hit him and threw him off to the concrete, crushing his spinal cord and several bones. If you don't know about spinal cord injury (SCI) the cardinal principle is not to move or turn the person until medical help arrives, and even after, all care must be taken not to move the spine. But in this case, all rules were violated. Two policemen lifted him and dragged him off to save him from the busy traffic. Soon he was lying in the intensive care unit of a trauma ward. Doctors, nurses, and attendants were rushing in and out with frightening whispers. In addition to his spinal cord injury, he had broken several bones. He writes in his blog: "I was having great difficulty in breathing and couldn't move my legs. In fact, I was not able to feel anything below the chest. I wished I were dead."

After a few weeks, he was transferred to a therapy facility. It was January 15, the day he was to travel to Switzerland, and he was lying in a bed undergoing occupational therapy. The therapist told him that her goal was to get him to attain "wheelchair independence.". He writes, "It didn't strike me immediately that what she was saying was that I won't be walking again in my life. When I thought about it a few minutes later, it was such a shock, that I was not able to react at all. I had to use all my will power to appear calm and smile, because my parents and my brother were with me. If I crumble they will also. So I smiled (if one can call that a smile) and asked her when do we start."

Slowly the sitting balance improved, and he was put on a wheelchair. Then they started teaching how to propel the wheelchair gracefully, how to do the transfers from bed to wheelchair, from wheelchair to car, etc. They also taught him to manage his daily activities: bathing, dressing, etc., like an infant starting to walk. From the rehabilitation center, he went to another hospital for a physical therapy treatment. There he had plenty of time to think, to plan, to rearrange priorities. He was living in a protected environment till then. Now, he had to face the real and harsh world, which even healthy people find difficult. Like every young person, Leon also had dreams— dreams about the future, about life, career, family, home, kids, etc. But everything was shattered to pieces on that fatal day. He began to collect those broken pieces and put them back into some sort of a shape. But the shape that came out was entirely different from the original one.

Leon says that he had never experienced the value of genuine friendship until then. He considers himself fortunate enough to have a very good friend who was with him throughout the entire ordeal. This friend traveled over one hundred miles regularly to bring him books, news, and other items that kept him occupied. Leon could share all his anxieties and fears, all his problems and pains to him. They began to discuss Leon's future aspirations. His close friends and family endured the pain along with him.

After spending nearly eight months in different hospitals, he decided to go back to work. His employer supported him by making arrangements and facilities to work sitting on a wheelchair. After a few weeks, the sores on his legs (due to continued sitting) made it impossible to continue work. So, he started a consulting firm with his brother and started working from home. During this time, he thought about writing. He read books about people who have struggled and succeeded against all odds. Those stories of courage, determination, and perseverance gave him hope. Almost four years after the accident, he is the partner and managing director of a successful software development company and has authored over twenty-four books. He has written books on technical subjects like computers, databases, career guidance, the Internet, Y2K problem, business computing, Microsoft Office, E-business, Software Configuration Management, and many others. He is also the coordinator and webmaster of Pegasus Book Club, an online book club on computing and information technology, management and business, engineering, etc. He also does technical evaluation of job candidates for many companies.

In the September 1994 issue of *Reader's Digest*, he read an article titled "Lessons my children taught me," by Chang Hsiao-Feng. In that article, she writes about adversity: "When God closes all doors, He opens a window. Often we spend so much energy banging on closed doors that we forget to feel and enjoy the breeze coming through the open window."

Leon now says, "Now I am learning to enjoy the breeze coming through the window. We are all fragile human beings with a short span of life. But God has a greater plan for each of us."

"But we have this treasure in jars of clay to show that this all-surpassing power is from God and not from us" (2 Corinthians 4:7).

Instead of asking, "If God exists, why is there so much evil or suffering?" we can ask, "If God doesn't exist, why there is so much beauty in the world?" If you feel like God is silent today, trust on what God is preparing for tomorrow. Has God trusted you with a silence? Remember, His silence is the sign that He is bringing you into a marvelous understanding of Himself. We can trust Him even when He is silent. We can learn to sing beautiful songs of joy and peace even amid the most troublesome and painful situations in life.

Printed in the United States
by Baker & Taylor Publisher Services

Printed in the United States
by Baker & Taylor Publisher Services